TOMORROWLAND

*A History of Western
Philosophy
by W T Jones, Vol. II*

Jeffrey M Jones

BROADWAY PLAY PUBLISHING INC
224 E 62nd St, NY, NY 10065
www.broadwayplaypub.com
info@broadwayplaypub.com

First printing: September 2007
I S B N: 0-88145-301-3

Book design: Marie Donovan
Word processing: Microsoft Word
Typographic controls: Ventura Publisher
Typeface: Palatino
Printed and bound in the U S A

TOMORROWLAND was originally produced
by Creation Production Company, opening on
6 September 1985 at the Performing Garage in
New York. The cast and creative contributors were:

TELEVISION STAR SHANNON MALLESON
  (*also* HUDRAY) . . . . Karla Barker
DIVINA WILFRED
  (*also* MISS PEGGY) . . . . Barbara Somerville
JASON WILFRED
  (*also* JIMMY RINGO) . . . . .Zach Grenier
SELDEN CLARK
  (*also* FRANK JAMES) . . . . .Gary McCleery
CAROL WILFRED
  (*also* MRS KENNISTON) . . . . Zivia Flomenhaft
DR CLIFF SINCLAIR
  (*also* LIBDER *and* DOC) . . . . .Victor Talmadge

Direction & set design . . . . Jeffrey M Jones
Sound . . . . .Daniel Moses Schreier
Costumes . . . . .Catherine Zuber
Lights . . . . Jeffrey McRoberts
Assistant direction . . . . .Jon Larson
Stage management . . . . Brad Phillips
Assistant stage manager . . . . Mary Bolton

NOTE

Virtually all dialog in this play has been constructed out of source material dating from the year 1950. Interested producers are hereby advised that certain texts used in this play may be protected by copyright law.

Permission for use of the sound score in this text must be obtained by writing Daniel M Schreier, 34 N Moore Street, #4E, NY NY 10013. All music indicated in the score is also obtainable from the same address.

DELRAY BEACH...just a typical Florida town,
...until the sun goes down....
...then it's *NEIGHBOR AGAINST NEIGHBOR*,
with *BLAZING TORCH* and *LASH*
and *HANGMAN'S ROPE!!!*

Men and women
dedicated
to what was to become a Lost Cause:
JASON WILFRED (A K A JIMMY RINGO)—
a head for figures...
...and a SUSPICIOUS MIND...
CAROL WILFRED (A K A MRS KENNISTON)—
just an ordinary housewife...
...OR IS SHE?
DIVINA WILFRED (A K A MISS PEGGY)—
she's behind the eightball...
...AND SHE DOESN'T EVEN KNOW IT!
SELDEN CLARK (A K A FRANK JAMES)—
Varsity quarterback, dream date...
...AND TROUBLE!
DR CLIFF SINCLAIR (A K A LIBDER and DOC)—
he thinks the Health Dept needs to know a lot more...
...ABOUT EVERYONE!
TELEVISION STAR SHANNON MALLESON
(A K A HUDRAY)—she's out of this world...
...IN MORE WAYS THAN ONE!

...so won't you join us as we visit:

the OFFICE of Doctor Cliff Sinclair...
the SUNPORCH of the Wilfred's magnificent,
new 1950 home...

and through the sunporch window,
the MOON, with the Earth rising!

(Sound: "Tomorrow Tone")

(The performance space is separated from the house by a pipe railing four feet high running the full width of the seating risers at the foot of the first row. White wall units twelve feet high divide the performance space into three areas.)

(The DOCTOR's office is defined by a six foot wall, set nine feet upstage parallel to the pipe rail, stopping three feet from the extreme stage left edge of the performance space to create an entrance. A small wood desk is placed in the center of the office; the doctor's chair faces the audience upstage of the desk, the patient's chair is downstage left of the desk, facing onstage. There is a microphone stand on the doctor's desk.)

(The sunporch of the WILFRED's beautiful, new, modern home is the main acting area. Stage left, it is defined by a six foot wall running upstage from, and perpendicular to, the onstage edge of the doctor's office. Four feet further upstage, a twenty-four foot wall runs parallel to the pipe rail, nineteen feet upstage of it, stopping five and a half feet from the extreme stage left edge of the performing space. A third wall extends six feet downstage perpendicular to the stage right edge of the second wall; a fourth wall extends four feet off stage right from the downstage edge of the third wall, running parallel to the pipe rail, stopping three feet from the extreme stage right edge of the performance space to create an entrance. The room is furnished with a table and four chairs center, fifteen feet upstage; and an easy chair eight feet upstage of the pipe rail, centered on the stage right wall. There are three place-settings at the table, S L, S R, and up center. A second microphone feeds from S R entrance.)

(The window is an aperture in the upstage right corner of the room, running from two feet to seven and a half feet high, extending eight feet towards center in the upstage wall, and two feet downstage of the corner in the stage right wall. Six feet upstage of the window are two masking units set at right angles, parallel to the corner of the room. The onstage unit, parallel to the pipe rail, is covered with a photomural showing earthrise from the surface of the moon. The other unit is covered with mylar and runs downstage from the stage right edge of the photomural, creating a mirror image.)

(Sound: a few minutes before curtain, as the audience is seated, SHANNON speaks over S R mike.)

SHANNON: Gyro control and compass O K...batteries all off...autopilot O K...everything's in order...pilot's ready...straight ascent from starting point...starting thrust using all tail assembly engines, 2300 tons...fuel mixture: hydrogen and oxygen plus A12, after 120 seconds hydrogen and oxygen plus A14, after 340 seconds hydrogen plus A16, after 560 seconds A16...
Radio and gyro compass in order...automatic pilot O K...fuel consumption normal...air pressure 15 pounds...
Stand by to turn...
Stand by...
4, 3, 2, turn...90 degree turn completed...ship on level flight...speed 3400 miles an hour...altitude 360 miles...three tenths of five left in tail section...
R X M calling Corplum...
R X M calling Corplum...
Hudray speaking...
We have leveled off at 360 miles altitude and are circling the globe at 3400 miles per hour. We will increase speed gradually until we reach escape velocity at 25,000 miles per hour. Everyone aboard ship well. Over to you...
5500 miles...continue acceleration...6,200 miles per

hour...altitude 1600 miles...speed 21,000 miles per
hour, constantly increasing...check pressurizing
system and oxygen...
Boy, this kind of weather makes me feel right at home....
24,000...stand by...25,000...prepare to jettison tail
system...start the front assembly motors...forty second
supply of fuel left...hold on tight, everybody...
R X M calling Corplum over to you...
We're on our way....
We have jettisoned tail section and are now reducing
power and speed according to plan until we come
within the attraction of the planet. This is probably
the last radio contact before return flight, everybody
aboard well....
R X M calling Corplum...R X M calling Corplum...over
and out...

*(Sound: crossfade to "Tomorrow Tone Long" and swell
lights: fade to black)*

PROLOG

SHANNON: *(On mike)* And now—
Let us turn the clock forward to the Robot Era of 2150....

With peace and reason ruling,
With vast numbers of highly developed robot machines
And with plenty of atomic and solar energy available,
What would life be like then?

*(Lights up in window. Window: flying saucer descends from
S L to S R.)*

SHANNON: The Sahara and other great deserts of today
   would be fruitful farmlands,
Irrigated by atomic energy and robot water services.
Humans would be happier, healthier, more energetic,
Living an abundant and secure life, with their wants
   satisfied cheaply by robot factories.
With a turn of the dial, the airwaves will become their
   servants,
Carrying entertainment from all corners of the world
   into their homes.
And almost every morning, winter or summer,
Jason and Carol Wilfred will waken to sunlight
   streaming through the pale-gray and aqua bedroom
Of their Delray Beach, Florida, home....

*(Room: lights reveal JASON in easy chair, reading the
Saturday Evening Post; DIVINA is beside him on the floor,
her head on the chair's arm. Sound: crossfade to "Lullabye")*

Scene One

DIVINA: Daddy?

JASON: Yes, angel?

DIVINA: What is a Cold War?

(Room: JASON *looks up from his reading, at audience.)*

JASON: *(Out)* Well, dear,
This odious phrase is used to describe a condition of
   enmity in which opponents are struggling with each
   other by every means except armed struggle;
Each, meanwhile, arming with ever more powerful
   weapons in anticipation of attack from the other,
And in the hope of deterring through fear such an
   attack.

DIVINA: But how does such a condition arise, Daddy?

JASON: It arises, dear,
When each believes—correctly or incorrectly—
That the other has ambitions incompatible with its own
   security and way of life.

DIVINA: Oh...

(Sound: swell "Lullabye," then fade back. Room: DIVINA
crosses to floor center, studying; then turns back to JASON.*)*

DIVINA: Daddy?

JASON: Yes, angel?

DIVINA: Is that belief under present circumstances
   justifiable?

JASON: Apparently so, angel.
Soviet Communists have always maintained,
And apparently sincerely,

That there will be no security for the Soviet Union so
   long as any—

(Sound: crossfade to "Gunfight")

JASON: —powerful part of the world remains
   capitalist—which,
In modern Soviet terms,
Means non-Stalinist.
The Soviet Union is therefore compelled by its basic
   theory to indulge in perpetual struggle with the
   non-Communist world....

(Room: fade lights. Window: SELDEN *as* FRANK *enters S R*
crossing center, followed by CAROL *as* MRS KENNISTON.
Sound: "Gunfight" swell, then fade.)

Scene Two

SELDEN: We lost em!

CAROL: Yeah, but you can't stay here, Frank—they'll be
   flushing these woods!
Can you ride?

SELDEN: Yeah, sure...

CAROL: Ah, no you can't!
You're hurt, Frank—you're hurt real bad.

(Window: SELDEN *turns to* CAROL.)

SELDEN: I'll be all right, Mrs Kenniston.
I think we better scatter anyway—
Best thing is every man for himself.
Best thing you can do is draw them away from here.

(Window: he crosses S R away from CAROL.)

CAROL: We're in this together, Frank—we stay together.
Must be a thousand posse men swarming this country!
You've got to hide out until things clear up a bit.

You're going to need a lot of care, and you can get it
  here.

(Window: CAROL *crosses to* SELDEN. *Sound: fade out*
"Gunfight")

SELDEN: Maybe you're right.
But how about the people here in this place?

CAROL: They think I went in to town shopping for the
  day.

SELDEN: That was smart....

CAROL: Be dark in a couple of hours...

(Window: CAROL *supports* SELDEN; *they exit S L. Sound:*
fade in "Mood 2")

CAROL: Come on, Frank—take it easy...

(Room: lights reveal JASON *&* DIVINA *as before.)*

Scene Three

DIVINA: Daddy?

JASON: Yes, angel?

DIVINA: Does scientific evidence make it appear likely
  that the hydrogen bomb can be made?

JASON: Well, dear,
The hydrogen bomb is theoretically possible.
The principles underlying it have been known to
  scientists here and abroad
For a number of years.

DIVINA: Do we know whether the Russians are working
  on the hydrogen bomb?

JASON: We have no reason to doubt they're working on
  all types of atomic weapons, angel.

DIVINA: Do we know if the Russians have produced the hydrogen bomb, Daddy?

JASON: I'm sorry, angel—
To answer that question would not be compatible with national security.

DIVINA: Well,
Do we know how advanced the Russians are in the development of the hydrogen bomb, Daddy?

JASON: Same answer, dear...

(Sound: swell "Mood 2", then fade)

DIVINA: Daddy?

JASON: Yes, angel?

DIVINA: Is there a danger that the hydrogen bomb could pollute the earth's atmosphere?

JASON: No...

(Sound: "The saint" button covers cut from "Mood 2" to "Slow Remorse." Room: fade lights. Window: SHANNON as HUDRAY enters S R, crossing S L while observing a hand-held "instrument." Presently, CLIFF as LIBDER enters S R.)

Scene Four

CLIFF: How are the others?

SHANNON: I think everybody's going to be all right.
Fortunately, the engines were turned off before we crashed.
I must have turned the levers off when I blacked out.

CLIFF: But at what speed?
You know the consequences of a body moving with unchecked velocity in free space!

SHANNON: So...?
We made a little detour.

CLIFF: How long has it been since—

SHANNON: I'm afraid we'll never know, Libder; but I've
   located them.

CLIFF: What?

(Window: SHANNON *crosses to* CLIFF.*)*

SHANNON: Corplum and the moon.

CLIFF: Well—where are they?

(Window: SHANNON *hands* CLIFF *"instrument".)*

SHANNON: Take a look.

CLIFF: But, Hudray, it can't be!
The instruments must have gone crazy!

SHANNON: No, Libder...I don't quite know how to tell
   you, but...

CLIFF: Yes? Yes?

SHANNON: Libder, if I could even have dreamed
That an incredible set of circumstances,
Each precisely and exactly timed,
Would carry us unerringly through space to our most
   congenial planetary neighbor,
Poskon—

CLIFF: Poskon?!

SHANNON: No doubt whatsoever...

(Window: CLIFF *crosses down S L.)*

CLIFF: But, Hudray...what does it mean?

SHANNON: It means, Libder, that there are times when a
   mere scientist has gone as far as she can.
(Window: she crosses down center.)
We must pause and observe respectfully while

something infinitely greater than ourselves assumes
  control.
I believe this is one of those times.

CLIFF: We shall go on, of course?

SHANNON: Certainly, we shall go on!
We should be betraying an unprecedented opportunity
  to do otherwise.
(Window: she crosses S L upstage of CLIFF.)
A day here is more valuable than years of research on
  Corplum.

CLIFF: Yes—of course, you're right....

(Window: as SHANNON *exits S L,* CLIFF *turns to follow.*
Offstage, CAROL *screams.* CLIFF *exits S L. Sound:*
CAROL's *scream, miked, covers cut from "Slow Remorse"*
to "Tomorrow Tone." Room: lights reveal JASON *and*
DIVINA *as before.)*

Scene Five

DIVINA: Daddy?

JASON: Yes, angel?

DIVINA: Did you ever kill anybody?

JASON: Nope.

DIVINA: Not even in the war, Daddy?

JASON: Just snakes...

(Room: CAROL *enters in bathrobe and curlers. Sound:*
CLIFF *over S L mike)*

CLIFF: "Disturbed Building..."

CAROL: Jason?

JASON: Yes, Carol?

CLIFF: *(On mike)* "Patients cared for in this building will
  be chronically disturbed,
Periodically uncooperative,
And assaultive on occasion...."

(Room: CAROL *points out window.)*

CAROL: There are creatures out there....

CLIFF: "Suicidal tendencies will be common,
And exceptionally close supervision will be
  necessary...."

(Room: JASON *rises, starts toward* CAROL.*)*

JASON: Are you sure you want Divina to hear this,
  Carol?

DIVINA: That's all right, Dad—I was just leaving.
(Room: she exits quickly S R.)

CAROL: Look...I'm not making this up—
I tell you, I saw them!
Right out there!
And when I yelled, they disappeared....

JASON: All right, Carol
(Room: he exits S L.)
Let's go see, shall we?

(Room: CAROL *crosses upstage to window; lights fade.)*

CAROL: ...And last night,
Things were answering me...

(Sound: swell "Tomorrow Tone" Room: CAROL *steps back
from window as, Window:* JASON *crosses S L to S R with
flashlight. Sound: "Thomas" button covers cut from
"Tomorrow Tone" to "Jazz Offbeats." Office: lights up
as* CLIFF *enters, with mike, to rail.)*

Scene Six

CLIFF: Hello, everybody!
My name is *(Your name here).*
In the story you are about to see,
I play the part of Doctor Cliff Sinclair,
Of the Delray Beach, Florida, Health Department.
(Room: he sits on edge of desk.)
The French *voyageur*, Jean Nicolette, was the first white
    man to come to Delray Beach—
That was in 1634.
Today, it is a flourishing business community in the
    heart of Florida's vacationland,
Noted for its paper manufacturing and cheese,
And famous to millions of Americans as the home of
    the Green Bay Packers.
Of course, our story is completely fictional,
And did not actually happen in Delray Beach,
Or anywhere else, for that matter.
Yet we came to Delray Beach in search of authenticity....

(Room: follow-spot picks up SHANNON *as she enters S R,
with mike, crossing behind chair down center to rail.)*

SHANNON: That's right, Cliff—
And during our stay, we fell in love with the
    small-town atmosphere,
The wonderful year-round warmth and sunshine,
The informal friendliness of the people.
Hello, I'm Television Star Shannon Malleson—

(Sound: "Applause" button. Room: SHANNON, *at rail,
crosses S R.)*

SHANNON: And on behalf of the entire company,
We salute the little community of Delray Beach,
And its citizens, who became our family....

(Room: CLIFF *and* SHANNON *point upstage to* CAROL, *who turns down from window in darkness.)*

CAROL: Family was large dark animal come roaring
    down the middle of...
My friends love books passionately...
Every kiss is fine....
(Room: she exits S L.)

CLIFF: A big family, Shannon,
That believes in the American way of life.
Folks that have never pulled down an 'Iron Curtain'
Between their hearts
And the Christian ideal called 'Brotherhood of Man'....

(Sound: "Applause" button. Office: CLIFF *sits behind desk, mike in stand.)*

CLIFF: So now, let's set the stage for our first Close-Up:
A Close-Up on Mister and Mrs Jason Wilfred
In their Delray Beach, Florida, home.
Shannon—Mrs Wilfred's your assignment.

(Sound: crossfade from Jazz Offbeats *to* Mood 2*)*

SHANNON: All right, Cliff—fine.

(Room: lights up as she crosses up to corner of window and sits on the sill, speaking into mike.)

Scene Seven

SHANNON: Yes, almost every morning, winter or
    summer,
Jason and Carol Wilfred waken to sunlight streaming
    through the pale-gray and aqua bedroom
Of their Delray Beach, Florida, home.

(Room: CAROL, *in housedress, enters S L and places salad bowl on table.)*

CAROL: It's the magnificent new 1950 home,
Beautifully decorated by Macy's,
The World's Largest Department Store.

(Room: SHANNON rises as CAROL crosses to easy chair and sits.)

SHANNON: From the hibiscus hedge comes the song of
    the mockingbird,
And the scent of gardenia drifts headily in the window.

CAROL: Because today,
The enjoyment of beauty is everyone's privilege.

(Room: SHANNON crosses center, upstage of table. Office: lights fade.)

SHANNON: Visitors to the Wilfreds' beautiful new
    modern home are impressed with evidences of wealth.
Designed by architect Richard Hanna,
It is striking enough in a community of beautiful
    ranch-type homes to attract half-a-dozen sightseers to
    the front door daily.

(Room: SHANNON has crossed to S L entrance; CAROL rises from easy chair.)

CAROL: And aside from being a beautiful, light, and
    airy house,
It is a miracle of easy housekeeping, Shannon,
(Room: she gestures, crosses center.)
With a complete line of Frigidaire home appliances
For pleasanter living,
For easier living,
For more economical living.

SHANNON: In fact...
(Room: she catches beachball tossed from S L entrance.)
Her daily routine is so well planned that Carol spends
    part of almost every day
At...the beach!
(Room: she tosses beachball to CAROL.)

CAROL: Yes! Winter temperatures in Delray average
  seventy-six degrees,
And in summer,
Gulf Stream breezes keep the mercury at a comfortable
  eighty.

(Room: SHANNON *has crossed down S R of* CAROL.*)*

SHANNON: I hear you're even getting interested in the
  Garden Club, Carol.

CAROL: That's right!
And you know... *(Sotto)* ...End-O-Pest provides all the
  pest protection most gardens need against chewing
  and sucking insects,
And fungus diseases, Shannon.

(Room: JASON *enters S L.)*

JASON: Evening, dear...

CAROL: Oh, hello there, dear!

(Room: CAROL *tosses beachball to* JASON *who tosses it off
S L while crossing to her S R side, as* SHANNON *crosses
further S R.)*

CAROL: Dinner'll be ready in just a few minutes—
Meat loaf and chocolate cake—
You and Divina can squabble over the last piece.
(Room: she puts arms around JASON's *neck.)*

JASON: Now that's the kind of close-in fighting I really
  enjoy, honey!
You see before you a man about to sit down to his
  favorite meal with his favorite family.

(Room: CAROL *puts her head on* JASON's *shoulder as*
SHANNON *speaks into mike.)*

SHANNON: Yes, just as soon as he can spurt home from
  work,
Jason's gray-blue convertible is parked outside their
  watermelon-pink front door,

For the Wilfreds are a spectacularly devoted and
   home-loving pair....

JASON: Can I give you a hand, dear?

CAROL: Just get everyone rounded up, please, dear—
I'll be right there.
(Room: she exits S L.)

SHANNON: A tireless personality with great drive...

JASON: *(Calling)* Divina!

SHANNON: And a range of interests that includes
   politics...

DIVINA: *(Off)* What?

SHANNON: Photography...

JASON: Dinner-time!

SHANNON: And modern architecture,

*(Room: JASON crosses S R, upstage of SHANNON,
to entrance; SHANNON follows behind him.)*

SHANNON: Jason is always delighted for an excuse to be
   with his family,
Although Divina—

JASON: Divina!

SHANNON: A charming and determined young lady...

DIVINA: *(Off)* In a minute, Dad!

SHANNON: Is the squeaky wheel that gets the grease, he
   says!

*(Room: SHANNON crosses down center as CAROL enters S L
with meat tray, crossing to table.)*

JASON: Hmmmmmmmm....
I wonder what's gotten into her?

*(Room: JASON crosses to S R side of table, as CAROL crosses
to S R entrance.)*

CAROL: Oh, she just has a lot on her mind, dear, that's all.

JASON: Yes, I'm beginning to think that she has.

CAROL: Divina—your dinner's waiting....

(Room: CAROL *exits S R as* JASON *crosses to easy chair and sits down.* SHANNON *at rail, center, on mike.)*

SHANNON: So, this is Delray Beach....

CAROL: *(Off)* Divina?

SHANNON: Not a fashionable resort,
But a small, friendly, forward-going American town,
Concerned with its churches and schools,
Band concerts and football teams—
The best kind of town, the Wilfreds feel,
To be found anywhere in the world.

JASON: Well, that's right, Shannon—
But you know, the defense of the United States is in a
    condition at which I am appalled.

SHANNON: Ladies and gentlemen, Mister Jason Wilfred.

(Sound: "Applause" button. Room: SHANNON *crosses to easy chair and sits on S L arm, holding mike for* JASON *to speak into.)*

Scene Eight

JASON: You see, an article in the current issue of the
    Saturday Evening Post has convinced me that if war
    should break out tomorrow,
We would suffer major initial disasters and be driven
    back on this continent to face a decade or a generation
    of desperate strife.

SHANNON: That's the current issue of the *Saturday
    Evening Post*
With the picture of *(Describe cover)* on the cover.

JASON: Of course, we wish to be strong so we can
    prevent war;
But the *Post* explains how, instead of appearing strong
    and resolute,
We are continually on the verge of appeasing,
And being alternately irresolute and desperate.
Shannon, no people in history have preserved their
    freedom
Who thought that by not being strong enough to
    protect themselves,
They might prove inoffensive to their enemies.

(Office: lights up as CLIFF *takes identical magazine from desk
drawer, and speaks on mike.)*

CLIFF: That's the *Saturday Evening Post,*
The magazine that hits the heart of America,
And certainly does in this article: "Is America
    Sleeping?"

JASON: I mean, I'd rather see an adequate radar defense
    network than a television set in every home,
Which seems to be about what we are going to get.

SHANNON: Thank you, Mister Wilfred.
*(Room: she rises, crossing behind chair to extreme S R side of
performance space to store mike.)*

JASON: Thank you, Shannon.

CLIFF: And thank you, Shannon Malleson.

(Sound: crossfade from "Mood 2" to "Tomorrow Tone")

Scene Nine

CLIFF: You know, folks,
As the season approaches when the occurrence of
    poliomyelitis threatens in some communities,
And mothers naturally become apprehensive,
We in the Health Department are asked literally
    hundreds of questions:
Shall I keep Jimmy home from the playground and the
    movie?
Is swimming dangerous?
In short: How can I protect my child from polio?

(Room: JASON *has crossed up to S R wall where he eyes*
SHANNON. *This dialog overlaps* CLIFF's.*)*

JASON: We have no tactical air force worthy of the
    name, Shannon,
And neither have our allies.
We had better get at it.

CLIFF: Unfortunately, we have to reply
That it is impossible to give answers which will be right
    for all children in all places.
Most mothers know, however,
That among children who get polio,
Those who have had tonsillectomies within the past
    few weeks are *twice as likely*
To get the deadly bubar type.
Children with bubar polio are in much greater danger.
So if symptoms appear, call the Health Department at
    once.
Do not take a child with these symptoms to a doctor's
    office.
If it is polio, you would thus endanger the others.

(Room: JASON *has moved close to* SHANNON *in
semi-darkness; his talking stops* CLIFF, *who glowers.)*

JASON: Now, the Russians have forty-thousand tanks, okay?
Many of these are heavy tanks, and among the best tanks in the world, by current measure.
Yet, there has been built and tested ammunition for a gun
Which can penetrate any armor a tank can carry!

(Sound: add "Jazz Offbeats." Office: CLIFF *cuts* JASON *off.)*

CLIFF: Only the doctors in your community are in a position to judge
Whether polio virus is present.

JASON: ...light, inexpensive guns,
Which can be used as squad weapons or carried in a Jeep!

CLIFF: So, by keeping in touch with the Health Department,
Mothers need have no great fear
As another polio season approaches.

JASON: Now, when a Jeep can meet a heavy tank and be a match for it, Shannon,
The day of the heavy tank is done.

(Room: DIVINA *enters S R, crosses up to* JASON *to give him a kiss, then to up center chair at table, where she sits; as* CAROL *enters behind her S R and crosses to S L chair and sits.)*

Scene Ten

JASON: Well...good evening!

DIVINA: I'm sorry, Dad.

(Sound: fade out "Tomorrow Tone." Room: JASON *crosses to S R chair at table and sits, as* SHANNON *moves to S R rail, on mike, in spot.)*

JASON: That's okay—we can wait—we always do....

SHANNON: Yes, Delray Beach is just a typical town....

JASON: What's gotten into you, young lady?

(Office: fade lights.)

SHANNON: Its houses are simple and largely of wood,
Painted white and surrounded by friendly lawns—
Those native shacks burning over there contained
   literature or guns or large stocks of rice....

(Room: JASON serves as DIVINA passes him plates.)

CAROL: So—did you have a nice day, dear?

DIVINA: Just wonderful, Mom—I mean...it was okay.

JASON: Just wonderful, hunh? Well, that means only
   one thing.
Who's the young man?

CAROL: Jason...

JASON: Oh, yes, I forgot, Carol—
Your little girl is saving herself for higher things than
   mere men.

SHANNON: To the right, the main street leads up a hill.
This is the business center.

DIVINA: All I said, Dad,
Was that the starry-eyed attitude about romance is so
   much schmaltz.

SHANNON: Elegant shops of men's and women's
   apparel,
Jewelry and leather goods,
Tempt you with their window displays.

CAROL: Could you pass the salt please, dear?...
Thank you.

SHANNON: But after dark, the loudspeakers begin to
   blare over the rice paddies,

Telling the people not to sell their rice to the
  government.

JASON: Well—Washington is playing Norton this week.

DIVINA: Don't worry, Dad—we'll wipe the floor with
  them.

CAROL: Divina, really.

JASON: No, Carol—we've got a fine team, all right.
'Course, the Coach ought to train that Selden Clark for
  defense as well—
We've got some holes there....

SHANNON: At the first turning stands the Health
  Department,
One of the most modern in America.
Further down are a school, a nursery, and a recreation
  center.
But every morning after dawn, patrols work over this
  road,
Looking for telltale signs of digging.

CAROL: So, I take it the staff meeting of the *News* went
  well, dear?

DIVINA: Pretty well, Mom.

JASON: Read your piece in the latest issue—not bad.
What's this one about?

DIVINA: Oh, nothing, Dad—real dull stuff.
It wouldn't interest anyone.

SHANNON: There is the inevitable drugstore with its
  soda fountain.

CAROL: Well, it doesn't sound dull to me, dear.

SHANNON: The movie—yes,
At the first superficial glance,
You wouldn't suspect the uniqueness of this town.
But then you notice the barbed wire fences.

The experiments which are conducted day and night
  behind those fences
Are America's most effectively guarded secrets.
(Room: she exits S R, with mike.)

CAROL: What did you say, dear?

DIVINA: I'm sure I haven't the faintest idea, Mom,
And could I please have the sunporch tonight,
Because Selden Clark is coming over to study.

CAROL: Why, darling—how nice—
Why don't you wear your new black velveteen?

DIVINA: Don't you think that's a little dressy for
  studying, Mom?
Anyway, I wouldn't have time—
Selden's coming over at seven-thirty.

JASON: Well, now—Selden Clark—
Maybe I could pass on to him some tricks I learned in
  my football days.

DIVINA: Actually, Mom, would you mind if I didn't
  finish?
I want to change and brush up a bit.

CAROL: Well, I think you ought to eat something....
Oh, go ahead, dear—
You can raid the refrigerator later....

(Room: DIVINA *exits S R Office: lights up,* CLIFF *on mike.)*

CLIFF: As a doctor,
I hear the things a son or daughter won't tell you.

CAROL: Well, I think it's wonderful....

(Sound: fade "Jazz Offbeats" out slowly.)

CLIFF: "Aw, gee, Pop—why can't we get a television
  set?"
You've heard that.

CAROL: Divina's been a—well—you know, so....

CLIFF: But there's more you won't hear.

CAROL: Well, anyway, I think it's very nice.

CLIFF: Do you expect your child to find words for the
   deep loneliness she's feeling?

JASON: They all seem clean-cut to you.

CLIFF: Do you expect her to blurt out the truth:
That she's ashamed to be with the gang,
Because she doesn't see the television shows they see?

JASON: Your anxiety to become a grandmother is
   warping your judgment, Carol.

(Sound: crossfade in "Low Rumble" slowly)

CLIFF: No, your daughter won't ever tell you the
   humiliation she's felt in begging those precious hours
   of television from a neighbor.

JASON: In my opinion, there's something the matter
   with him.

CLIFF: And yet, you give your child all the sunshine and
   fresh air and vitamins you can.

CAROL: Why do you say that?

CLIFF: What about sunshine for her morale?

JASON: There's always something the matter with them.

CLIFF: What about vitamins for her mind?

JASON: That's the only kind she's interested in.

CLIFF: Doctors agree—
Television is all that and more for a growing child.

CAROL: She's maternal, that's all.

CLIFF: You see,
Social competence is a big force in any child's life;
And today, it is practically impossible for boys and girls
   to

"Hold their own" with friends and schoolmates unless
  television is available to them.

JASON: Probably marry some weakling, just so she can
  mother him.

CAROL: She won't! And, Jason—
You stay out of the sunporch tonight.

CLIFF: So, take it from me—
When television means so much to your child,
Can you deny it to your family any longer?

(Window: SHANNON *leans in at down S R corner,
with mike, in spot. Office: fade out lights.)*

SHANNON: Then, across their laughter, tragedy struck!
And revealed in Carol depths of fortitude she never
  knew existed!
While driving Jason to work one morning
When the roads were slippery with wet leaves,
She skidded and stalled and was hit broadside by
  another car!
(Window: she leaps off, S R.)

CAROL: The car in front of me just seemed to poke along.
Although I am normally a careful driver,
I lost patience, and just as we were approaching a hill,
I took a chance.
As I pulled alongside...

(Window: SHANNON *enters S R, as before.)*

SHANNON: Her own car was demolished, and Carol a
  broken heap on the floor,
With her teeth jarred loose,
All her ribs on one side broken,
And a broken back!

CAROL: The car in front of me just seemed to poke along.
Although I am normally a careful driver...

JASON: Actually, dear, would you mind if I didn't finish
   either?
I've got some business to attend to myself.

(Sound: crossfade from "Low Rumble" to "Big Country")

SHANNON: Then, across their laughter, tragedy struck!
(Window: she leaps off, S R.)

JASON: Things are going on in this territory that are
   suspicious and mysterious.
The men keep bringing in reports of wagon tracks—
Three times in the past week, wagon tracks—
But nobody ever sees any wagons.
Well, I intend to get to the bottom of it.
(Room: he rises and crosses back around chair to window.)
I'm sending a patrol out to Comanche Territory to look
   for signs of Indian migrations.

CAROL: Comanche, dear?

JASON: Maybe Comanche, maybe Setank.

CAROL: Setank, dear?

(Room: JASON puts foot on windowsill at S L edge.)

JASON: Kiowah chief, honey—big medicine man—
He's worse than Comanch.

CAROL: Well, I've never had a dinner fall apart on me
   quite this fast before, but
Go ahead, dear—
(Room: she rises and crosses to JASON.)
I'll save some chocolate cake for you.

*(Room: CAROL exits S L with two plates JASON holds out
his hand in window, and an arm extends from S L side of
window with cowboy hat, which he takes and puts on.)*

JASON: And another thing, Carol.
Those two Indian braves in the guardhouse,
Convicted of running guns to the Indians?

CAROL: *(Off)* Yes, dear?
(Room: she enters S L with tray, clears table.)

JASON: Send a detail to carry out the sentence of the
    court.
They're to be executed and their bodies buried outside
    the post—at once, Carol!

CAROL: Yes, dear.

JASON: This thing's dragged on for months.

*(Room: JASON exits S L; CAROL continues to clear Office:
CLIFF exits S L. Sound: crossfade from "Big Country" to
"Mood 2")*

Scene Eleven

CAROL: Goodness—I wish Jason wasn't so fussy.
Always wants his orange juice just squeezed—and he
    means just!

*(Window: SHANNON enters S L with two glasses of orange
juice.)*

SHANNON: Have you ever tried serving him Bird's Eye
    Orange Juice, Carol?
Tastes better than just-squeezed—and takes only
    forty-five seconds to fix!
Just add cold water and shake—wow!—what juice!

CAROL: Don't tell me this is frozen orange juice?
Tastes better than just squeezed—
Or any frozen juice I *ever* tasted!
Believe me, Shannon—
I'll never be talked into taking anything but Bird's Eye!

SHANNON: And for meal that's good and doesn't take
    time, Carol—

(Window: SHANNON is handed plate of chicken from S L.)

SHANNON: Serve Bird's Eye Fried Chicken Paprika!
It's wonderful, and takes less than forty minutes.
You see—Bird's Eye chicken comes ready for the skillet.
(Window: she holds plate up; chicken is glued on.)

CAROL: And every bird's a best bird, Shannon—
A plump and juicy young bird!
It's the tastiest chicken I ever sailed into!

SHANNON: Well, you know, Carol,
When I serve Bird's Eye Fried Chicken Paprika at my
    famous little suppers,
(Room: she steps over S L windowsill to enter.)
Celebrities beg me for the recipe!

*(Room: SHANNON and CAROL squeal with excitement,
then sit: SHANNON up center, CAROL S L, at table.)*

SHANNON: But now, living in Florida as you do,
You also enjoy salad meals all year round, don't you?

CAROL: Well, yes, we do, unh-hunh....

SHANNON: In fact, I understand you have an interesting
    philosophy about salads.

CAROL: That's right.
We hardly ever have the same salad twice, Shannon.
(Room: she turns out to audience.)
(Out) Ours is a basic salad, you see, with variations,
Like a basic fashion wardrobe with accessories.

(Sound: crossfade from "Mood 2" to "Jazz Piano Trills")

SHANNON: Isn't that interesting?
And how does that work on a daily, uh—

CAROL: Well, Jason and I collaborate on it.
I'm the V P, or Vegetable Preparer, Shannon—
I have everything ready,
And then Jason presides over the dressing and tossing.
I must say, Jason has very definite ideas about salad
    dressing.

SHANNON: He certainly does, Carol—
But you know, folks, having tried it,
I think Jason has a mighty good idea worth trying in
   anybody's salad.

CAROL: Well, I'm sure he'd be glad to hear you say so,
   Shannon.

SHANNON: Well, good...

(Window: JASON *as* JIMMY RINGO *enters S L crossing S R;
behind him,* CLIFF *enters S L as* DOC.)

Scene Twelve

CLIFF: Ain't you heard?

JASON: Heard what?

CLIFF: Everybody in town's talking about the hold-up.

SHANNON: Of course, greens are the ground work for
   any tossed salad.

CAROL: That's right.

CLIFF: They figure maybe it was Frank James....

(Window: JASON *turns to* CLIFF.)

CAROL: I prefer to use romaine and lettuce.

JASON: Did you say Frank James?

CLIFF: That's what they say—
And you can get ten thousand dollars for him,
Dead or alive.

CAROL: And then for variety, I'll add...

JASON: ...Frank James...

CAROL: ...well, in fact, anything I've prepared:
Tomatoes... Sliced cucumbers... Radishes...

JASON: What's he doing around here, Doc?

CLIFF: Comanche Territory's crawling with Indians,
  Jimmy.
(Window: he crosses S R to JASON.)
Supposing his mission is to lead an armed uprising?
All he has to do is gather up a few thousand men and
  call them soldiers....

CAROL: Slivers of cheese... Cubes of cooked meat... Raw
  spinach leaves...

(Window: CLIFF crosses behind JASON up S R.)

CLIFF: 'Course, Frank James gets blamed for everything.

JASON: You never lived in Comanche Territory, Doc.
You couldn't possibly know the kind of people we had
  to deal with:
Bushwhackers—murderers—
Frank James shot down women and children in cold
  blood, Doc.
And I'm going to get that outlaw if it's the last thing I
  do.
(Window: he crosses S L.)

CAROL: Sometimes I'll even add sliced cooked beets to
  please Jason,
Although I don't care for them myself.

CLIFF: That may take some doing....
(Window: he crosses down S L to JASON.)
They say he's away—in Comanche Territory.

JASON: Oh, he's away, all right, you may be assured of
  that.
But he'll return.
And when he does, I'm going to get him.
Oh, he's got spies everywhere, yes.... but so have I.

(Window: JASON crosses up behind CLIFF S R; CLIFF turns
to follow him.)

JASON: They tell me he's kind of a natural man.
Say he don't look too different from a lot of fellows.
See, you can tell a snake by his shape and a skunk by
 his stink, but an outlaw...? Well,...
You cain't tell an outlaw by his face,
But he's somebody's next door neighbor.
So you watch for him—listen for him—
Memorize, remember, study every suspicious scrap of
 talk—
Because you will recognize him, not by his face,
But by the unmistakable odor of his words.

(Window: DIVINA *as* MISS PEGGY *enters S R crossing up behind* JASON.*)*

JASON: The stench is un-American!
(Window: JASON, *sensing someone behind him, wheels and draws on* PEGGY*; beat, then laughs and tips his hat.)*

Scene Thirteen

JASON: Miss Peggy...

(Window: DIVINA *crosses down to* JASON.*)*

DIVINA: Going hunting, Mister Ringo?

(Window: JASON *exits behind* DIVINA*, S R.)*

JASON: Man hunting...

(Window: CLIFF *follows* JASON *off S R, behind* DIVINA*, as he exits he twirls his cane.)*

CLIFF: Ma'am...

(Sound: crossfade from "Jazz Piano Trills" to "Mood 2." Window: DIVINA *watches men exit, turns and exits S L.)*

Scene Fourteen

CAROL: *Tuesday*, Shannon, we'll have a big steak or
   chops with the salad, if the budget's ahead that week,
   which more than likely it isn't, so I'll do something
   with hamburgers,
Which we like in all manner of ways....

SHANNON: Unh-hunh...

CAROL: A kind of chile is our favorite.
Wednesday is our casserole day—
Even in hot weather, Jason wants something hot and
   filling—
I've never been able to get away with serving a salad as
   the main attraction,
No matter how appetizing and decorated it may be.

SHANNON: Unh-*hunh*...

CAROL: Now, Thursdays are my off-the-record days.

SHANNON: No work.

CAROL: No work.
In the afternoons I take care of a Brownie Girl Scout
   troop,
Maybe go shopping,
So dinner has to be truly quick and easy that night,
   Shannon.
(Out) Now, to me, this one is it,
And what's more, it satisfies a hungry husband.
I buy the frozen sandwich steaks and take them out of
   the freezer compartment at noon.

(Room: CAROL *freezes as* SHANNON *says:)*

SHANNON: When Carol was about ten,
She overheard an adult say:

What a pity she's such a plain child, when her baby
   sister is so beautiful.

CAROL: We like them on toast with pan gravy.

(Sound: crossfade from "Mood 2" to "Slow Remorse."
Room: CAROL *freezes as* SHANNON *says:)*

SHANNON: After that, Carol understood why,
When she came to her mother with her face streaked
   with tears,
Her mother would jeer:
You're your father's child—go to him—go away!

CAROL: And I usually have ice cream and chocolate
   sauce on hand.

(Sound: add in "Jazz Piano Trills." Room: CAROL *freezes as*
SHANNON *says:)*

SHANNON: Her wealthy, spoiled mother would not
   tolerate anything around her that was not beautiful.

CAROL: The sauce is the real, old-time kind.

(Room: CAROL *freezes as* SHANNON *says:)*

SHANNON: "She had the money and she called the
   shots," Carol recalls feelingly;
And she can vividly remember painful scenes over
   money between her mother and her handsome, West
   Point father,
From whom she learned the virtues she practices today.

CAROL: They used to serve it hot over ice cream when I
   was a youngster—
It drips down all over the ice cream and sort-of hardens.
We love it.

(Room: CAROL *freezes as* SHANNON *rises and says:)*

SHANNON: After that, she was rarely home with her
   quarreling family.

(Sound: cut out "Jazz Piano Trills")

SHANNON: It still hurts to remember, however,
The time she came down with typhoid when her
   mother was planning a lavish dinner party for her
   younger sister.
"Oh, Carol," exclaimed her mother, "how tiresome of
   you.
Go to your room and lock your door."
(Room: she crosses S L with juice glasses.)
None of the guests at the gay dinner party that evening
Suspected there was typhoid in the house.

*(Room: SHANNON exits S L. SELDEN as FRANK JAMES
enters S R.)*

Scene Fifteen

SELDEN: You know why I come here, don't you?

CAROL: I guess I do.

SELDEN: How is she?

CAROL: Fine.
(Room: she rises and continues clearing table.)

SELDEN: I want to see her, Mrs Kenniston.

CAROL: You think she wants to see you?

SELDEN: Where can I find her?

CAROL: I'm afraid I can't tell you that, Frank.

SELDEN: What do you mean, you can't tell me?

CAROL: All right, then—won't tell you.
(Room: she exits S L with tray.)

SELDEN: Why?

CAROL: *(Off)* Because nobody here knows who she is,
   Frank.
She's got another name now, and another life.

(Room: she enters S L with sponge.)
And it looks to me like that's the way she wants it to
    stay.

(Room: SELDEN *crosses to S R edge of table.)*

SELDEN: How'd you like to see that street out there full
    of gunplay?

CAROL: I'd rather not.

SELDEN: Well, that's probably what you'll have in a
    couple hours.
(Room: he sits in S R chair at table.)
'Cause I ain't leaving here till you get a hold of her for
    me.

CAROL: And what if she don't want to talk to you?

SELDEN: You let her do the decidin' about that.

CAROL: Will you go, then, if I tell her?

SELDEN: Just leave it to her—that's all I ask.

CAROL: I'll see what I can do about it.

(Room: CAROL *exits S L with last of table settings.*
Office: lights up as CLIFF *enters S L and sits behind desk,*
looking through file. JASON *hovers in entrance.)*

Scene Sixteen

CLIFF: Won't you come in, please, Mister Wilfred?
My name is Doctor Sinclair.
So—you're concerned about your wife?

(Sound: fade out "Slow Remorse" to silence. Office: JASON
enters, crosses down around chair to rail.)

JASON: Our family doctor gave me your name, Doctor.
And he said, "I don't take cases like Carol's anymore.
But you go and call the Health Department,

And they'll tell you what's wrong and what to do about
   it."
I hope you don't think I'm always as jumpy as this,
But this is not easy for me, Doctor.

CLIFF: Naturally, these things aren't easy for the
   families of the patients.
Won't you sit down, Mister Wilfred?

(Office: JASON *sits in patient's chair, S L.)*

JASON: Thank you.

(Office: CLIFF *rises and perches on S L edge of desk.)*

CLIFF: Now, tell me,
How long has it been since you first noticed anything
Peculiar
In your wife's actions?

JASON: Doctor...
Everything I tell you is confidential, isn't it?

(Blackout)

(Sound: "Saint Descent." Room: SELDEN *exits. Office:
lights reveal* CLIFF *sitting behind desk, writing in file;*
JASON *in S L chair.)*

Scene Seventeen

JASON: ...Well, our paths crossed at Saks' one day when
   she tangled up a sales check—
I made a few sarcastic remarks about her addition,
And she replied she wished she had never left Klein's
Where the customers were all gentlemen.
She was completely spoiled,
But even so we clicked immediately.
She struck me like a small package of dynamite.
That very evening, I asked her to a party,
And seven weeks later we were married.

CLIFF: I see. Please, go on.

JASON: Well, we honeymooned in Maine, visited friends
in Vermont,
Moved to New Haven where I got an excellent job with
the Bell System doing statistical research....

CLIFF: Yes...

JASON: Then, across our laughter, tragedy struck....

CLIFF: Mmmmmmmmm... Tell me, Mister Wilfred?

(Sound: slow fade in of "Hymn Drone")

JASON: Yes, Doctor?

CLIFF: Do you have any trouble at the time of
intercourse?

JASON: Why, no, I—don't think so, Doctor....

CLIFF: No pain, or...

JASON: Not particularly...

CLIFF: The experience is satisfactory, you could say?

JASON: Yes.
I think so.

CLIFF: Good.
Please continue, Mister Wilfred.

*(Office: lights fade. Sound: swell "Hymn Drone;" SHANNON
on S R mike, off. Window: spot on earth glows brighter.)*

Scene Eighteen

SHANNON: *(Off)* And now,
Let us turn the clock forward to the Robot Era of 2150.
With peace and reason ruling,
With vast numbers of highly developed robot machines,
And with plenty of atomic and solar energy available,

(Sound: add "Slow Remorse")

SHANNON: What would life be like then...?

*(Sound: cut out "Hymn Drone." Window: lights up,
DIVINA as MISS PEGGY enters S R crossing up, followed
by CAROL as MRS KENNISTON; they both look down S L.)*

Scene Nineteen

DIVINA: Did you ever see anything so terrible in your
  life?
It's like the whole town's gone crazy.

CAROL: He's here to see you, you know.

DIVINA: Have you seen him?

CAROL: I just left him.
Why don't you see him, if only for a few minutes?

DIVINA: Oh, Mrs Kenniston—what good would it do?
(Window: she crosses down center.)
It's over now, you know that.

CAROL: Not for him.
(Window: she crosses down center, S R of DIVINA.)
He's still crazy about you, Peggy.

DIVINA: He was crazy about me before, but that didn't
  stop him from being the kind of person he was.
(Window: she turns S R to CAROL.)
He scares me, Mrs Kenniston—he really does.

CAROL: He might have scared you then, but not now.
He's different.

DIVINA: How different?

CAROL: The way Bucky was different that last year. You
  know—
(Window: she takes DIVINA's arm.)
Not wild any more, just sorry.

(Window: DIVINA *turns away from* CAROL.*)*

DIVINA: And what good did that do Bucky?

CAROL: None, I guess.... But I liked it.

(Window: DIVINA *turns back to* CAROL.*)*

DIVINA: Oh, if only he'd stayed away!

(Window: CAROL *turns to* DIVINA.*)*

CAROL: Is it somebody else, Peggy?

DIVINA: No, of course not—you know it's not!

CAROL: Not Jimmy Ringo?

(Window: DIVINA *backs away S L.)*

DIVINA: Jimmy Ringo—why do you ask that?

CAROL: Is it?

DIVINA: I'd never even thought of Jimmy like that.

CAROL: Of course not.
You think he never thought of you like that?

DIVINA: I doubt it... Jimmy's just... Well, Jimmy's just
  Jimmy.
Oh, really—you must be out of your mind!

(Window: she turns, crosses S L to corner. CAROL *crosses
S L behind her.)*

CAROL: Then it's still Frank, isn't it?

DIVINA: I guess so.
I guess it always will be.

(Window: CAROL, *her arm around* DIVINA, *leads her off S L;*
SHANNON, *with mike, leans in down S R, in spot.)*

Scene Twenty

SHANNON: *(Out)* Are you always lovely to love?...
Suddenly...breathtakingly...you'll be embraced...
    kissed...held!
Perhaps tonight.
Be sure then that you are always lovely to love...
Sweet and alluring...
Never uncertain...
Try Stopette,
The deodorant in the amazing squeezeable bottle.
Hello, again, I'm Television Star Shannon Malleson,

(Sound: "Applause" button covers cut from "Slow Remorse"
to "Mood 2." Room: SHANNON *enters over S R sill,*
passing mike back off through window, and crosses center.)

SHANNON: With a very special message for all you
    older teens,
Brought to you by Stopette,
The deodorant in the amazing squeezeable bottle.
Because, whether you know it or not,
You've changed a lot, girls—
And now is the time to start taking all that big-gal
    attention in your stride!
So... When a boy jumps to his feet as you come in the
    room,
Or holds your drink in a hamburger hangout—
That's a compliment.
And when he makes like a miler to open the car door
    for you,
That's a compliment, too.
Just remember—
All it takes is a smile from you to make him feel
Able as Gable and
(Room: she makes a "V" sign.)
Twice as lucky!

(Room: SHANNON *exits S R. Office: lights reveal* CLIFF
sitting at desk, JASON *in S L chair, his head in his hands.)*

Scene Twenty-one

JASON: ...then, after weeks in the hospital,
Carol was brought back home in a Bradford brace—
A steel spine,
With claws to catch her shoulders and a belt to go about
  her middle!
Once in it she was helpless to go out or do anything
  except barely totter around.

(Sound: slow fade out of "Mood 2" to silence)

JASON: When I left in the morning, I would belt her in,
And all day she would sit,
Watching the cars go by,
The pressure of the brace becoming increasingly
  intolerable until she was in tears of agony when I
  came home...
For eight months she endured this, Doctor—
Trying to distract her mind from the pain and the
  loneliness by reading cookbooks—
The basis, no doubt, of her excellent herb cookery today.

CLIFF: I'm sorry, Mister Wilfred—
But in this case it would be a useless gesture to expend
  the time and talents of valuable therapists when their
  energies can be directed towards individuals with a
  more favorable
Rehabilitation Potential classification.

(Sound: fade in "Telephone Ring" low)

JASON: Is she in danger, Doctor?

CLIFF: It could be....

(Room: DIVINA *enters S L with books, crosses to window.)*

CLIFF: I'll be frank to say I think she's in danger of something.

(*Room:* CAROL *enters S L, watches* DIVINA.)

CLIFF: So, we'll make no more guesses until we've had an opportunity to find out, shall we?

(*Sound: slow fade in of "Jazz Off Beats." Office: lights fade. Room: lights up*)

Scene Twenty-two

CAROL: Your young man is a little late, isn't he, dear?

DIVINA: Mom, for heaven's sake—don't call him "your young man."
(*Room: she sits at table, center.*)
He's only coming over to study.
I wish everybody wouldn't act like we were going steady.

(*Room:* CAROL *crosses S R behind* DIVINA.)

CAROL: You know, Divina—
When a boy spurns you, or seems to,
It is not necessarily a reflection on you.
It doesn't prove that you're a flop.
You can't click with everyone you meet.
(*Room: she sits at table in S R chair.*)
That would prove you were a malleable clay dummy,
Who pushed and pulled her personality into shape to match everyone else,
Not a flesh-and-blood girl,
With definite ideas of her own.
So if Sheldon or whoever-it-is—

DIVINA: Selden, Mom...

CAROL: Yes, dear.
So if Selden, the boy you think is so wonderful,

Wants to take somebody else to the dance,
It's futile to go over everything you said and did.

DIVINA: Jeepers, Mom—do you mind?
I'm trying to get a little work done!

(Room: CAROL *rises, crosses behind* DIVINA's *chair.)*

CAROL: Would you like a cookie, dear?

DIVINA: No, thank you, mother.

CAROL: Some chocolate cake?
Studying always made me hungry.

DIVINA: No thanks.

CAROL: There's orange juice.
Some orange juice?

DIVINA: Thank you, mother. That would be very nice.

CAROL: *(Out)* Bird's Eye Frozen Orange Juice!
It's bound to be better!

(Room: CAROL *exits S L;* SHANNON *enters S R, smoking.
Sound: cut out "Telephone Ring")*

Scene Twenty-three

SHANNON: Of course, poise is a big part, too, of acting
    your age.
You see, boys like girls who seem at ease because that
    makes them feel more relaxed, too.
(Room: She crosses to S R side of table, gives DIVINA *her
cigarette as she takes off gloves, etc.)*
But often, on those big evenings,
When both the date and the dress are new,
Poise can be slow to come....

DIVINA: And how!...
Say, Shannon—what was that formula you were telling
    everybody about for getting a boy interested in you?

SHANNON: Oh, that...
(*Room: she takes cigarette, puffs, takes a bow off her own hair and ties it around* DIVINA's.)
So why the sudden interest, Divina?
Could it be that you hanker after that Selden Clark?

(*Sound: crossfade from "Jazz Off Beats" to "Hootenanny"*)

DIVINA: Well, I wouldn't put it that way, exactly.
But he is one of the nicest boys I ever met, I will say that.

SHANNON: Oh, he's glamorous, O K—
And he plays football like a dream.
So that's why you've been walking around in a daze
    lately.
(*Room: she crosses to S R chair and sits.*)

DIVINA: Well, I don't see why you're so surprised.
Ever since he transferred to the High, every other girl in
    the Senior Class has been—darn it!

SHANNON: But he'd be wonderful for you, Divina.

DIVINA: Well, I wasn't planning on taking him as a
    tonic.
But I'm glad you approve—
He's coming over tonight.

SHANNON: Over here? Tonight? You minx—what a
    triumph!

DIVINA: Save your raves for the stag line, Shannon.
He fell all over me in the library this afternoon.
He had Latin to do and so did I—
Then he got snowed under, somewhere around *veni,
    vidi, vici,*
And anyway, I helped him,
And he's coming over tonight for more.

SHANNON: Well, don't cry about it, for heaven's sake!

(*Room:* DIVINA *rises.*)

DIVINA: Oh, Shannon—do you think I should have
  worn my new black velveteen?
Do you think I should mention football to him?
Do you think I have too much lipstick on?

SHANNON: Hey—calm down, Divina—take it from me:
What guys really go for are sweet-smelling Stopette
  girls.
(Room: she rises, producing small bottle.)
You see, I use Stopette myself,
And so I recommend it to all my fans.
Just an effortless squeeze of the Stopette Flexi-Plastic
  bottle does it all.
And Stopette carries the Good Housekeeping Seal of
  Approval,
So you know it's safe, as well as effective.
This smaller size—purse or travel size, I call it—
Contains up to six months supply, and sells for just
  sixty cents plus tax.

DIVINA: But Shannon—
Here I am practically desperate with Selden Clark
  coming over,

(Window: SELDEN crosses S R to S R, with books.)

DIVINA: And all you do is yakkety-yak about Stopette!

SHANNON: Play smart, Divina—
Never risk offending others needlessly.

DIVINA: Gee... Maybe you're right.

*(Room: DIVINA takes the bottle. Sound: "Doorbell" button
covers crossfade from "Hootenanny" to "Mood 2.")*

DIVINA: Oh, jeepers—there he is—I've got to run!
*(Room: she crosses S L, then back to SHANNON to give back
the bottle, then exits S L.)*

SHANNON: *(Out)* How about you?
Are you sure of your present deodorant?

Ask yourself:
Are you always lovely to love?

(Sound: SELDEN *and* DIVINA, *offstage, on S R mike. Room:*
SHANNON *exits S R.)*

Scene Twenty-four

DIVINA: *(Off)* Hiya, Selden...

SELDEN: *(Off)* Oh, hi, Divina...

DIVINA: *(Off)* How are ya?

SELDEN: *(Off)* Yeah... I mean, fine—
How are you?

DIVINA: *(Off)* Oh, okay, I guess....

(Sound: crossfade from "Mood 2" to "Piano Suspense."
Office: lights reveal CLIFF *sitting behind desk;*
JASON *rises from patient's chair and bangs desk.)*

Scene Twenty-five

JASON: It's no use, Doctor!
I just can't take it any more!

CLIFF: Look, Mister Wilfred—
You don't have to do this, of course,
But if you do, you'll know that you've done everything
  humanly possible to keep your marriage intact.
If you don't,
You're going to wake up one night and say to yourself:
Maybe this would have made the difference.
Maybe Carol could have become the woman she was
  when I married her.

(Office: JASON *sits down again, S R chair.)*

JASON: Operate, you mean?

CLIFF: That's right—right away.
There's no time to be lost.

JASON: And you can't tell me anything more definite
    about it?

CLIFF: I'm afraid I cannot.
If the problem is attacked vigorously at this time and
    properly coordinated,
With first things coming first,
It can be put in satisfactory condition in a few years.
If she drifts as she is going,
It will remain in unsatisfactory condition,
And may well lead to disaster.
Can we reach her by telephone, Mister Wilfred?

(Sound: slow fade out of "Piano Suspense" to silence)

JASON: Yes. She's at home now.

CLIFF: Good.
(Office: he rises.)
You get her and tell her I'm coming right over.
Don't worry, Mister Wilfred.
You're doing exactly the right thing.

*(Office: CLIFF exits S L; fade lights. Room: SELDEN enters
S L with books, DIVINA following; SELDEN crosses S R to
window corner; DIVINA crosses S R to up center chair at
table.)*

Scene Twenty-six

DIVINA: Well, I'm glad you found your way without
    any trouble.

SELDEN: Yeah—sure was nice of you to let me come,
    Divina.
I was really in deep trouble this afternoon.
Guess I'm not the Latin type.

DIVINA: Oh, it's not so bad, once you catch on.

(Room: SELDEN *crosses down S R to easy chair.)*

SELDEN: *Hic, hac, hoc—*
Why do they make us learn this stuff, anyway?

DIVINA: But don't you feel as if
Your friends, and the books you read, and the music
   you listen to,
As if they all become a part of you?

SELDEN: Well, yeah, I suppose some people look at it
   that way,
But football and baseball and so forth,
They're more important to me, I guess.
(Room: he turns to face DIVINA.*)*

DIVINA: Guess I just couldn't imagine living without
   books.

SELDEN: Yeah.
Guess I never thought of it that way, particularly.
I don't get to read too much.

DIVINA: Yeah.

SELDEN: Pretty swell layout you got here.

DIVINA: Yeah, it's nice.

SELDEN: You're kind of bashful, aren't you?

DIVINA: A little.
(Room: she crosses down to SELDEN.*)*

DIVINA: Most everybody is, you know.
You're more self-conscious than I am—
That's why you act as forward as you do.

SELDEN: Yeah. So—um,

(Room: by advancing on DIVINA, SELDEN *backs her up S L
to table.)*

SELDEN: Are we going to study in here?

DIVINA: Well, sure, if that's okay—
There's a table right over here.

(Sound: fade in "Fiddle")

SELDEN: Yeah.
So, where were we?

(Room: DIVINA slips around table to up center chair, taking S R chair with her around corner and putting it S R of center chair.)

DIVINA: Right here...

(Room: DIVINA sits center, opening books as SELDEN crosses and sits in S R chair, opening books. Office: JASON rises from S L chair and crosses far S R at pipe rail, in spot, as: Window: CLIFF, as DOC, enters up S L and crosses S R, leading CAROL as MRS KENNISTON center.)

Scene Twenty-seven

JASON: *(Out)* You know Frank James, don't you, Mrs Kenniston?

CAROL: More or less, I guess.

JASON: What do you mean, more or less?
You either know him or you don't.

CAROL: I only know him by sight, Jimmy.

(Rail: JASON turns up to face CAROL.)

JASON: But you were there when this thing happened—
Didn't you recognize him?

CAROL: How could I?
They wore masks.

JASON: Yes, we know that they were masked, Mrs Kenniston,

But you could still give us a physical description,
  couldn't you?

(Sound: crossfade from "Fiddle" to "Cowboy Train")

CAROL: Well...he's got two hands, like everybody else...
I'm sorry, Jimmy—
It all happened so fast, and then I got scared and ran.

(Rail: JASON *turns out to audience.)*

JASON: The truth of the matter is,
You people are all scared to death of that outlaw.

CAROL: If you were living around here before the war,
You'd be afraid of him too, Jimmy.

JASON: I was here before the war—remember?

CAROL: Then you ought to know what happens to
  people who turn in an outlaw.

JASON: Mrs Kenniston, this is not Comanche Territory—
This is a law-abiding community,
And we won't have Frank James running wild through
  our streets,
Shooting and killing our women and children.

CAROL: He ain't exactly running wild through our
  streets.

JASON: When I want your opinion, Mrs Kenniston, I'll
  ask for it.
This is an outrage—
Frank James literally running wild through our streets—
(Rail: he turns back to CAROL.*)*
Of course, you can't say for sure it was Frank James.

CAROL: That's right.

JASON: In fact, you can't even say for sure that it wasn't.

(Sound: crossfade from "Cowboy Train" to "Fiddle")

CAROL: Why, no—no, I can't.

JASON: Well...
Getting you to admit that was quite something.

(Rail: JASON *starts to cross back S L in spot. Window:*
CLIFF *crosses down to* CAROL *and leads her off, S R.)*

JASON: Thank you, Mrs Kenniston.
That's good enough for me.

(Office: JASON *exits S L. Room: lights fade brighter;*
SELDEN & DIVINA *as before, studying at table,*
S R and center respectively on upstage side.)

Scene Twenty-eight

SELDEN: ...8 and 4 is 12, put down 2 and carry 1...

DIVINA: If you don't mind—
A differential 6 over M to the 30th power...
The half-way check result is:
262 thousand to 341 thousand both using tangent E.
Correct?

SELDEN: Uh....
That isn't the result that I have....

(Room: DIVINA *takes* SELDEN*'s paper.)*

DIVINA: It must be the same.
I have to say that you've made an error and discard
   your figures.

(Sound: add "Slow Boogie-Woogie")

SELDEN: I didn't make any error.

DIVINA: You made a mistake in your addition.

SELDEN: I did not!
(Room: he rises and crosses up S R to window corner.)

DIVINA: There's an error there, Selden—I'm sorry.

SELDEN: Why bother saying you're sorry?

DIVINA: Surely you're not going to let emotion enter into this?

SELDEN: No.

DIVINA: Then we'll continue computing using my results as a basis.

(Sound: add "Tomorrow Tone." Room: SELDEN turns to face DIVINA.)

SELDEN: Hey—why can't you be more like a girl? Nothing but work, work, work—can't you ever relax?

DIVINA: Oh, and I suppose you think women should only cook and—

(Room: SELDEN sits at table in S R chair and "studies.")

DIVINA: And, and sew and bear children.

SELDEN: Well, there's such a thing as going overboard in the other direction, too, you know.

(Office: SHANNON enters S L and sits at desk.)

SELDEN: ...Never suspected you knew so much about everything...

DIVINA: ...At least I'm well mannered....

(Sound: fade out "Slow Boogie Woogie" and "Fiddle" from "Tomorrow Tone" Office: lights up; SHANNON on mike.)

Scene Twenty-nine

SHANNON: Stand by for a special announcement.
At four o'clock this morning,
North Korean armed forces began unprovoked attacks
  against defense positions of the Republic of Korea
At several points along the 38th Parallel.
Fighting is now in progress along the Parallel.
Both Korean officials and the security forces are

handling the situation calmly and with ability.
There is no reason for alarm.
As yet, it cannot be determined whether the northern
  Communists intend to precipitate all-out warfare.
Mission personnel are advised to travel about as little as
  necessary.
The Ambassador requests that Mission personnel
  remain at home or at their posts,
As the situation may dictate.

(Sound: crossfade from "Tomorrow Tone" to "Jazz Piano Trills")

SHANNON: Our next announcement will be heard
At three o'clock this afternoon.

(Office: lights fade; SHANNON exits S L, with mike. Room: JASON enters S L, crossing down S R to easy chair to sit as CAROL enters S L crossing S R to table with plate of cookies; SELDEN rises.)

Scene Thirty

JASON: *(Reading)* So...how are things at the Brain Factory?

DIVINA: Just fine, Dad.

CAROL: Are you two making any progress?

SELDEN: Oh, yes, thanks—Divina's a real brain.

DIVINA: Mom—Dad—this is Selden Clark.

(Room: DIVINA rises; CAROL places cookies S L on table and reaches S R behind DIVINA to shake SELDEN's hand.)

CAROL: How do you do, Selden?

SELDEN: How do you do, Mrs Wilfred.

(Sound: add "Telephone Ring")

JASON: *(Without looking up)* Good evening, Clark.

SELDEN: Good evening, sir.

CAROL: Well, I thought you two might enjoy a snack. Studying always made me hungry....

SELDEN: Me, too—say, these cookies look swell.
(Room: he crosses S L behind DIVINA to cookies.)

CAROL: Just help yourself—there's more if you want them, Selden.

(Room: SELDEN crosses back to S R chair at table.)

CAROL: And cold fresh orange juice.

DIVINA: Orange juice, Selden?

SELDEN: Oh, yes, thanks.

CAROL: And how about a slice of chocolate cake?

SELDEN: Gee, I'm supposed to be in training, but... Sure—O K.

(Room: CAROL exits S L.)

SELDEN: That's sure nice of your mother, to go to all that trouble.

DIVINA: Oh, Mom loves to cook.
(Room: she sits at table in center chair, motions to SELDEN to sit again.)
Besides, have you noticed how bad the meals have been getting in the cafeteria lately?

(Room: SELDEN sits at table in S R chair.)

SELDEN: I'll say—they're sure crummy.

CAROL: *(Off)* I'll get it!...

(Sound: cut out "Telephone Ring")

SELDEN: All the fellows on the team are complaining about it.

(Sound: CAROL *offstage on S L mike)*

CAROL: *(Off)* Hello?...

DIVINA: You know, Dad used to be quite a football
  player in his day, too.

CAROL: *(Off)* No, this is her mother....

SELDEN: Yeah, I know.

CAROL: *(Off, not miked)* Divina!

SELDEN: Coach talks about him all the time.

CAROL: *(Off, not miked)* It's for you, dear....

DIVINA: Will you excuse me for a moment, please?

SELDEN: Sure...

(Room: DIVINA *exits S L)*

CAROL: *(Off, not miked)* Anyone else for chocolate cake?

(Room: JASON *puts down his magazine.)*

JASON: Well...speaking of the team, Selden,
How do you feel about next Saturday?

(Sound: DIVINA *offstage on S L mike)*

DIVINA: *(Off)* Hello...?

SELDEN: Oh, okay, I guess, Mister Wilfred...

DIVINA: *(Off)* Listen, Shan—the situation here is critical!

SELDEN: We worked out a couple tricky plays at
  practice tonight.

DIVINA: *(Off)* We are endeavoring to build up the force
  necessary to hold the enemy, but to date our efforts
  against his armor and mechanized forces have been
  ineffective.

(Room: JASON *rises, pacing first slowly S L, then upstage by
S L wall of room.)*

DIVINA: Our own troops are fighting with valor under
  overwhelming odds of more than ten to one,
But the Army is entirely incapable of counteraction,
And there is grave danger of further breakthrough.

(Sound: crossfade from "Jazz Piano Trills" to "Jazz Offbeats")

JASON: Right—but I think the backfield is your main
  worry.

DIVINA: *(Off)* All indications are the situation is
  disintegrating so rapidly we may not be able to get
  out.

(Room: JASON *crosses S R behind* SELDEN *to window.)*

SELDEN: Well, you could have something there, Mister
  Wilfred.
But don't you worry about Norton.
They've got a green team—it'll be a cinch.

DIVINA: *(Off)* Was considerable fighting around East
  Gate and Chongno areas...

JASON: Well, maybe Norton, but...

DIVINA: *(Off)* Resistance combined police and Army...

JASON: ...Ridgefield is something else again.

DIVINA: *(Off)* ...overcome by Wednesday noon.

JASON: Take last Saturday.

DIVINA: *(Off)* All prisoners killed immediately.

JASON: If you'd been playing Ridgefield,
You'd have been sunk on that end play.

(Sound: add "Tomorrow Tone" to "Jazz Offbeats")

DIVINA: *(Off)* There is no fighting now in Seoul.

SELDEN: How do you mean?

(Room: JASON *crosses behind* SELDEN *to table, center, and
draws on* DIVINA*'s paper.)*

JASON: Well, look—now this was how the play was set
   up...
You see...?

DIVINA: *(Off)* All People's Army forces preceded by
   tanks in every advance;
Enemy soldiers surprisingly young and small
   compared our Army,
Heavily armed with tommy guns....
Captain Sinh says fight will all be over by this
   afternoon....

JASON: ...so, you see—
If that pass had gone wild and been intercepted,
You'd have left yourself wide open....
(Room: he crosses S R behind SELDEN *and exits S R.)*

DIVINA: *(Off)* In meantime has turned over full
   authority to Chief Army Staff and radioed people to
   remain indoors and calm when tanks arrive.

SELDEN: Say, you're right about that, Mister Wilfred.

DIVINA: *(Off)* He says will stay in Seoul with Army
   Command to end.

SELDEN: I'll talk to Coach about it first thing in the
   morning.

DIVINA: *(Off)* He despaired of saving anything...
I made no commitment...

(Sound: fade out "Jazz Offbeats" from "Tomorrow Tone")

DIVINA: Yes, I'll let you know, but I'm sure there isn't a
   chance...
....Goodbye....

(Window: JASON *as* JIMMY RINGO *enters S R, crossing S L.)*

Scene Thirty-one

JASON: You're Miz Kenniston's new hired man, ain't you?

SELDEN: That's right.

JASON: You been coming here a lot.

SELDEN: Well—sick horse.

JASON: How sick?

SELDEN: Well, I don't know....

(Window: JASON *crosses back S R.)*

JASON: Say, come to think of it—
That horse don't look too sick at all.

(Room: SELDEN *rises crossing S R to face* JASON.*)*

SELDEN: Look, I only work for Miz Kenniston, Mister.

JASON: You sure about that?
I'm thinking maybe Frank James gives you your orders.

SELDEN: Frank James? Who's he?

JASON: How long you lived around here?

SELDEN: Eight months.

(Sound: slow crossfade from "Tomorrow Tone" to "Low Rumble")

JASON: Then you're a liar—
Because no man can live in Delray Beach and not know Frank James.

(Room: SELDEN *crosses to rail down center.)*

SELDEN: I don't get into town so much.

JASON: You were in town yesterday.
You were in Bergdorff's saloon.

SELDEN: All right.

JASON: You had a beer there with another fellow.

SELDEN: Yeah—old friend of mine.

JASON: Old friend of yours...
(Window: he crosses S L; puts foot on sill.)
Now, they took pictures of them outlaws—doggone if
  one of them didn't look just like that friend of yours....

SELDEN: Naw...Steve Brill?
Why, he works on a farm over in Comanche Territory.
He and I come from the same town.

JASON: Oh, you lived in Comanche Territory before you
  came here?

SELDEN: That's right—I was born there.
Everybody knows me.
(Rail: he turns upstage to face JASON.)
If you don't believe me, why don't you ride on over
  and ask them?

JASON: Well, maybe I will.
Sorry to have bothered you

(Window: JASON starts to exit S L as DIVINA as MISS PEGGY starts to enter S R; as, Room: SELDEN starts to cross up to window as CAROL, in nightgown, carrying tray with orange juice, starts to enter S L; Sound: swell "Low Rumble;" All characters freeze as, Room: SHANNON runs on S R crossing center in spot.)

Scene Thirty-two

SHANNON: Wrong?!
Yes, they were wrong—but, remember:
They lived in a Time of Violence and an
Age of Strife.
Men and Women Dedicated to what was to become a

Lost Cause.
Some called it War.
But in Delray Beach it was worse than war—
It was neighbor against neighbor with blazing torch,
And lash,
And hangman's rope!

(Room: SHANNON *exits S L. Window:* DIVINA *moves
S L toward* JASON.*)*

Scene Thirty-three

DIVINA: Jimmy?

JASON: Why, good evening, Miss Peggy.

DIVINA: Jimmy, what's all this talk we hear that it's
    Frank James stirring up the Indian with promises that
    they'll have this land back when the war is over?

(Room: CAROL *crosses to table, sets tray S L.)*

JASON: Well, figure it out for yourself, Miss Peggy.
At any time, Setank could throw a thousand braves
    against us.
Fortunately, that's not the Kiowah way—
They raid and run.

(Window: DIVINA *turns away, S R.)*

DIVINA: Oh, why do you men like to fight?
For hatred? For killing?

JASON: No, ma'am—the war's most particular to me.

(Window: JASON *crosses S R to* DIVINA, *behind her. Sound:
crossfade "Low Rumble" to "Slow Remorse")*

JASON: But the war's a long way off—least it seem so
    round here:
Let's keep it that way, shall we?

CAROL: Orange juice, Selden?

JASON: That's a beautiful dress.

SELDEN: Oh, thanks, Mrs Wilfred.

DIVINA: What makes you say that?

CAROL: Want to pour yourself one?

JASON: I was merely trying to pay you a compliment,
  Ma'am....
(Window: he looks back down S L.)
Yup—real Southwest night...

SELDEN: How long were you going to keep it up?

CAROL: Keep what up?

SELDEN: Keep watching me from the door.

(Window: DIVINA *also looks back down S L.)*

DIVINA: "Blemishes are hid by night,
And all our faults forgiven...."

SELDEN: It was making me nervous.

(Room: CAROL *crosses center, toward* SELDEN.*)*

DIVINA: The world should live by night, Jimmy.
Dark draws people together—they can feel the need for
  each other....

CAROL: You're very attractive when you're nervous,
Frank,

(Window: DIVINA *crosses S L in front of* JASON.*)*

DIVINA: But the world gives the night for the
  sick—keeps for itself daylight—
That lets men look into faces filled with fear and hatred.
Are you filled with fear and hatred, Mister Ringo?

JASON: All the time, Ma'am.

CAROL: Come on—let's dance.

(Window: JASON *crosses to* DIVINA *as, Room:* CAROL
crosses to SELDEN.*)*

DIVINA: Then you're bound to be a great man one of these days, aren't you?

CAROL: It's been a long time for me.

SELDEN: Say, I ought to go and find Divina, Mrs Wilfred. She kind of wandered off.

(Office: CLIFF *as* LIBDER *enters stealthily S L, beckons to* SHANNON *as* HUDRAY *to follow him; they watch the room as, Room:* SELDEN *steps past* CAROL *and crosses up S L to exit until she stops him by saying:)*

CAROL: Don't go!

JASON: You know, you've been a great deal in my thoughts, Miss Peggy,
Even when I didn't see you.
They say that thoughts, like time, can't stand still....

(Room: CAROL *crosses to* SELDEN; *whispers:)*

CAROL: This was on the arrow:
Blue follows the Green.
The Gray is under the Blue.
The Red is to the right of the Green.
The Gray must go five leagues to the point of 8,
And then return seven leagues to meet the Red.
I want you to know, Frank.
I understand why you are on your guard.

DIVINA: But time can stand very still, Mr Ringo.

(Room: CAROL *crosses down S R to easy chair and sits.)*

CAROL: How long are you staying here tonight?

SELDEN: That all depends.

CAROL: Depends on what?

DIVINA: Good night, Mister Ringo.
(Window: she exits S L.)

SELDEN: Good night, Mrs Wilfred.

(Room: SELDEN *exits S L. Office:* SHANNON *has crossed S R behind desk.)*

Scene Thirty-four

SHANNON: Beautiful...
The mind that conceived this must have been of a high
  order of intelligence.

CLIFF: At least the equal of Corplum...
Perhaps considerably above ours.
To think that complex organized society existed here
  once.

(Office: SHANNON *crosses S L to* CLIFF.)

SHANNON: Yes, ironic, isn't it?
The mind, wherever you encounter it—Corplum or
  Poskon—
The highest attainments of the intellect always diverted
  to self-destruction.
(Office: she crosses down to rail, S L.)
What a lesson for our world!
One blast—thousands of years of civilization wiped out!

CLIFF: But there's always the possibility of a meteor.

SHANNON: No, this is definitely blast coupled with
  extreme heat.
Perhaps the entire surface of the planet is one vast ruin.

CLIFF: Maybe now I can convince you to go back to the
  ship.

SHANNON: No, we can't stop now—
We must find out what kind of creatures they are!
(Office: she exits S L.)

CLIFF: But we don't know how many there are—and
  supposing they're hostile?
A blast like this—I should hate to think that anyone

survived.
We still don't know all the genetic effects of radiation,
But that it will produce mutations, malformations,
    disfigurements— blindness—
(Office: he exits S L.)
(Off) That much we're sure of from research!

(Window: JASON *turns upstage to his left as* SELDEN
as FRANK *enters S R crossing up.)*

Scene Thirty-five

JASON: Listen, stranger—I'll make a deal with you.
You tell me where he is, I'll see you get the money,
Every single dollar of it.

(Room: DIVINA *enters S L crossing to table to straighten
her books.)*

SELDEN: I don't know what you're talking about.
I never saw Frank James in all my life.

DIVINA: In case you didn't know it, Mother,
You're looking at the social flop of the year!

(Window: JASON *crosses S R to* SELDEN.*)*

JASON: You're lying.

(Room: DIVINA *runs down S R to easy chair and puts her
head in* CAROL'*s lap, crying.)*

DIVINA: The first chance he got, he galloped out of here.

SELDEN: You know so much, what are you wasting
    your time with me for?

DIVINA: Oh, brother, how dumb can a girl get?

SELDEN: Why don't you go out and get him?

JASON: I don't know where he is—I told you that.

DIVINA: She's behind the eightball, and she doesn't
  even know it.

SELDEN: Well, you won't find him where he was
  yesterday,
That's for sure.

DIVINA: Do you think I'm happy?

JASON: That I know.

DIVINA: I'm not happy.

*(Sound: crossfade from "Slow Remorse" to "Big Country
Short")*

SELDEN: You'll never get him alive, either.

DIVINA: I'm so confused, I—
(Room: she runs off S R.)

JASON: Who said anything about getting him alive?
I gave up that idea years ago.

*(Window: JASON exits S L. Sound: swell "Big Country
Short;" SHANNON on S L mike.)*

Scene Thirty-six

SHANNON: *(Off)* And now, let us turn the clock forward
To the Robot Era of 2150!
With peace and reason ruling—
With vast numbers of robot machines
And with plenty of atomic and solar energy available
What would life be like then?....

*(Window: SELDEN [as FRANK] turns S R as DIVINA [as
MISS PEGGY] enters S R and runs to him and kisses him.
Sound: fade down "Big Country Short." Room: CAROL rises
from easy chair, crosses slowly up center to table.)*

DIVINA: It's funny—
We've been together such a short time,

And yet it feels like it's been forever.
I don't know....
When we're not together, I—
I feel like I'm suspended in midair,
With nothing down beneath except the end of the
  world.
I love you so much, Frank.

(Room: CAROL *crosses guardedly S L to entrance; stops;
then backs away S R to up center chair at table.)*

SELDEN: Your cheek is burning—you're a bundle of
  nerves.

DIVINA: Don't be my doctor—not tonight—
Just hold me tight—so tight I can't get away from you.

(Room: JASON *enters S L crossing S R to table.)*

SELDEN: You're not about to get away from me—
I'll never let you get away.

CAROL: What is it, Jimmy?

JASON: The post is under siege, Mrs Kenniston.

*(Sound: crossfade from "Big Country Short" to "Big
Country Long")*

CAROL: Setank?

JASON: Yes, Setank—they've got us surrounded.

CAROL: How many would you say?

JASON: About twelve to fifteen hundred.
But they ain't attacked yet.

CAROL: They never do at night.

(Room: CAROL *crosses S L around table to* JASON. JASON
turns away from her, down S R.)

JASON: Go on—why don't you say what you're
  thinking?
Say we've got to surrender.

Say there are women and children here.
(Room: he turns back to CAROL.*)*
Tell me they're Americans!
Tell me if the post is wiped out it'll be because—

(Room: JASON *turns away,* CAROL *reaches to turn him around again,* JASON *kisses her.)*

DIVINA: Oh, Frank, I want to get away from here,
I want to get out of this part of the country,
See if we can't find a little ranch, maybe—
He'll kill you, Frank—I know he will!

SELDEN: But he doesn't even know about us, Peggy.

(Room: JASON *drops to his knees in front of* CAROL.*)*

JASON: I'm sorry, Mrs Kenniston

SELDEN: I tell you he doesn't even suspect!

JASON: Better get down and get some feed, Ma'am,
That's about all I can think of for the present.

(Room: CAROL *kneels down next to* JASON. *Sound: crossfade from "Big Country Long" to "Big Country Short" and swell.)*

SELDEN: You don't have to worry about me, Peggy.
I can take care of myself.

(Room: CAROL *lies on floor and pulls* JASON *down on her.)*

JASON: I've told the men to carry on their assignments....

DIVINA: And what about me, Frank?

JASON: Patch up as best they can...

DIVINA: Every time your man leaves the house, you
wonder when he's coming back.

JASON: In a way, I don't suppose it matters....

DIVINA: Every time there's a knock on the door, your
heart stops!

JASON: You know what we're in for in the morning.

(Room: CAROL *rolls over on top of* JASON.*)*

DIVINA: Every time you pick up the paper, you're
   afraid.

SELDEN: Peggy, stop it!

JASON: Try and keep it from the children if you can.

DIVINA: You're afraid you'll find he's dead!

(Window: DIVINA *runs off S R;* SELDEN *starts to follow.)*

Scene Thirty-seven

CAROL: *(To* JASON*)* No, wait, Frank—leave her alone!

(Window: SELDEN *stops, turns momentarily, then exits S R.)*

CAROL: I didn't want any of these people to get hurt.
They've been good to me, Frank—
Especially Jimmy Ringo and the girl!
They mustn't be hurt, no matter, Frank—do you
   understand?

(Room: JASON *throws* CAROL *off him.)*

CAROL: Why do you think I've been protecting
   you—covering up for you—lying for you?
I didn't know what I was getting involved in when I
   saw the hold-up!
Then I found out you were involved and I kept quiet!
But not any more—
I'm through covering up—
I'm gonna identify you, Frank!

(Room: CAROL *embraces* JASON; *he pushes her away.)*

JASON: Oh, my god, Carol—you don't even know what
   you're saying—you don't even know what you're
   saying—
You're so desperately sick!

CAROL: You are!

(Room: JASON *gets up and backs away up S R.)*

JASON: No—you are—you, Carol! All the symptoms!
I didn't marry a woman: I married a mental disease!

*(Sound: cut out "Big Country Short" and fade in "Planets."
Room:* CLIFF *enters S L, crossing to* CAROL *as: Office:*
SHANNON *enters S L with mike.)*

SHANNON: *(On mike)* Ruptured?...

CLIFF: My name is Doctor Sinclair, Mrs Wilfred.

SHANNON: ...Get relief this proven way...

CLIFF: I'm with the Health Department and I'm here to
  help.

SHANNON: Get back to normal living with this new
  appliance innovation that lets you
Run, play, work, lift, stoop or squat,
Like any normal person.

(Room: CAROL *gets up and crosses to* CLIFF.)*

SHANNON: No leg straps, no elastics, no plastics...

CAROL: Then you heard.

SHANNON: ...Flex-O-Pad...

CAROL: Why pretend you hadn't heard?

SHANNON: ...Entirely different...

CAROL: That television, what they said over that
television it was...

SHANNON: And a degree of comfort you never thought
  possible.

CLIFF: Is that what your husband was trying to tell me,
  Mrs Wilfred?

(Room: CLIFF *leads* CAROL *S R to easy chair where she sits;
as* JASON *crosses S L behind table and sits in chair at center.)*

SHANNON: Light...inexpensive...guaranteed...

CAROL: Of course he was trying to tell you!

SHANNON: ...Delay may be serious...

CAROL: Do you think he's the only man who ever found
   me attractive?

*(Room: CLIFF shakes a small bottle of serum and fills a
syringe.)*

SHANNON: ...Order today...

CAROL: Mr Jason Wilfred doesn't have any feelings!

JASON: No, I have feelings, Carol.
I have pity.

CAROL: Pity!
Nobody pities me!
Nobody pities me, nobody! Nobody!

*(Room: CLIFF injects CAROL as JASON pours a glass of juice.
Sound: slow crossfade from "Planets" to "Tomorrow Tone")*

CLIFF: Easy, Mrs Wilfred, easy...
This will make you feel better.

*(Room: CAROL sinks back in easy chair as CLIFF turns
upstage and crosses to window corner, back to audience.)*

Scene Thirty-eight

CAROL: That night the weather moved in and clouds
   came down and it began to pour....
I wanted to get to Delray Beach.
But word came that it had fallen into enemy hands.
Through the window, I could see nothing but swirling
   gray clouds and moisture slipping like soft jewels
   against the glass.
Two hours out...

CLIFF: Did you make it clear to her that we suspected
    her of passing information on to Setank?

CAROL: ...the clouds suddenly began to break up....

JASON: Yes.

CAROL: And we could see the roads below us,
Black with people headed south.
Then trains appeared—crawling along a single track....

CLIFF: And what was her reaction?

CAROL: ...all headed south and covered with people.

JASON: ...She seemed surprised and said:
I do not think so.

CAROL: After we landed at Delray,
Something caught my eye in the sunlight.

(Room: CLIFF *turns and crosses to S R edge of table, leaning
on it with both hands.)*

CAROL: The leading edge of the wing was in flames.
The rubber encasing the de-icer was burning and
    spurting little orange curls of flame.
The plane seemed doomed....

CLIFF: Did you make it clear to her that we were in
    possession of precise information on this matter?

CAROL: ...so I waited for her to explode....

JASON: ...Yes.

CAROL: ...but she didn't—
At least, not right away.

CLIFF: ...And what did she say to that?

CAROL: And except for the little orange flames and
    some smoke curling up from the pilot's window,
Everything seemed quiet.

JASON: She again said: I do not think so.
Perhaps you will tell me what the evidence is.

(Room: CLIFF *crosses S L behind* JASON *and around S L edge of table, to pour himself a glass of juice.)*

CAROL: By this time, it was getting along toward sunset,
   and we could see the fire inside glowing brighter,
   when all at once,
The cabin fire burned through the windows and up
   through the astrodome and gushed into the cockpit,
   and the nose burned off, and then the great tail flukes
   rose slowly against the evening sky as the right wing
   tanks exploded....

CLIFF: ...And this remained her attitude?

JASON: Yes...

CAROL: ...And even as that beautiful old plane died,
The evening sky turned from old rose to blood red,

(Room: CLIFF *sits down in S L chair at table.)*

CAROL: And flares ignited by the blast fell through the
   belly of the ship and lay burning on the runway,
Their greens and scarlets reflected by the glistening
   undersurface of the wings.
Through it all...

JASON: ...I don't know who's the guiltier

(Sound: swell "Tomorrow Tone" and add "Kiss Drum")

CAROL: ...as soft umbrellas of flame opened around the
   plane...

JASON: ...The one who commits the crime;
Or the one who just stands by and does nothing about it.

CAROL: ...other fires began to burn....

CLIFF: ...Sometimes I sit around for hours trying to
   figure that one out.

CAROL: And tiny stars of incredible intensity showered out of the inferno and lay shimmering and dancing around the ship....
As died the fire...

JASON: ...I mean,
Here we are looking for a bunch of outlaws....

CAROL: ...So died the sunset....

JASON: And when we find them, who will they be?

CAROL: ...And it was cool and dark....

JASON: ...Probably friends of ours...

CAROL: And night lay upon the land

CLIFF: Complicated, isn't it?

(Blackout)

(Room: as lights fade, CLIFF *crosses down S R to* CAROL *in easy chair.* CAROL, CLIFF *and* JASON *exit in blackout. Window: earthglow reveals* SELDEN *as* FRANK JAMES *at S L corner loading pistol. Sound:* SHANNON *on S R mike)*

Scene Thirty-nine

SHANNON: *(Off)* And now...
Let us turn the clock forward to the Robot Era of 2150,
And see what life would be like then....

(Sound: cut out "Tomorrow Tone" leaving "Kiss Drum" to swell. Window: SHANNON *enters S R with mike in spot.)*

SHANNON: Good evening, sir.

SELDEN: Ma'am.

SHANNON: Mighty windy country.

SELDEN: This ain't even a breeze.

SHANNON: Pretty hot.

SELDEN: Wait till summer.

SHANNON: Really?

SELDEN: If we live that long.

SHANNON: And how much time do you think you have
  left?

SELDEN: Oh, we're all right as long as them smoke
  signals is there.
It's when they stop that I'm going to sweat.

SHANNON: Well, cheer up—look—there's more smoke
  over there.

SELDEN: Oh, this ain't going to be no picayune affair,
  Ma'am.
Looks like Setank's rounding up the whole tribe.
And that dust there now—
There's a war party underneath that just as soon as
  you're born.
Don't strain your eyes, Ma'am—
They'll be there tomorrow.
If I know these Indians,
And I ought to,
We're going to see a lot of them before too long.

SHANNON: And what are you going to do about it?

SELDEN: Well, a man who knows this country might be
  able to bust through if he could get by their patrols—
After dark, of course—
'Course, they're just waiting for us to try it—
That's why they got the patrols out there.
And they can afford to lose a few men—we can't.

SHANNON: But you know this country—couldn't you
  make it?

SELDEN: Not with a woman tagging along.
I tell you,

I don't mind the sniping, but I sure could do with a lot
   less of them drums!

(Sound: cut out "Kiss Drum," reveal "Indian Raid")

SELDEN: You reckon them buzzards left something
   around here?

SHANNON: Looks a little like they don't believe you're
   leaving.

SELDEN: Never did like them things studding on me.
'Taint because the buzzards know what they're doing.
But it brings to mind the question:
Do I know what I'm doing?

SHANNON: And your name again is...?

SELDEN: Oh, I'm a stranger here, myself, Ma'am....
(Window: he crosses S L, stops, turns back to her.)
I'm a long way from home, and I can't afford to make
   any mistakes.

(Window: SHANNON exits S R.)

SELDEN: I think nobody has been so far from home as
   me.

*(Office: in darkness, CLIFF enters S L and sits behind desk;
CAROL in bathrobe enters S L and sits in patient's chair, S L.
She puts S L mike in stand. Sound: SHANNON on S R mike)*

Scene Forty

SHANNON: *(Off)* Take a good look at this man....
If you saw him fishing at a summer resort,
Would you be able to tell what he does for a living the
   rest of the year?
Is he a letter-carrier?

(Window: SELDEN exits S L.)

SHANNON: A movie talent-scout?
A tugboat captain?
What would you do if he turned to you and said:

ALL: *(Off)* What's...My...Line?

(Sound: cut from "Indian Raid" to "Clip Clop." Room:
SHANNON *enters S R with mike in spot, crosses center.)*

SHANNON: From C B S Studio 51,
Hughes-Farady Incorporated, makers of Stopette
  deodorant,
The deodorant in the amazing squeezeable bottle,
Brings you television's sensational new game:
What's My Line?
Once again tonight, we're going to put our cameras
  close up on a few people from some varied and
  perhaps unexpected occupations,
And to start things rolling,
It's time to meet our first challenger—
So won't you come in, sir, and sign in please!

(Sound: cut out "Clip Clop;" fade in "Planets." Room: fade
out spot. Office: lights reveal CLIFF *and* CAROL.)*

Scene Forty-one

CAROL: I've been bleeding.

CLIFF: Badly?

CAROL: No, I wouldn't say badly. Just a little...

CLIFF: I see.

CAROL: Every day.

CLIFF: Um-hmmmm...
Then the flow is profuse, you would say.

CAROL: Well, I don't know.

CLIFF: I see.
Tell me, Mrs Wilfred,
Have you had any pain along with this bleeding?

CAROL: No, not very much.
I'm just a little sore and sensitive.

CLIFF: Look, Mrs Wilfred—don't hold out on me—
I was able to feel it plainly during my examination:
A soft boggy mass about the size of a plum,
And extremely sensitive,
As you well know.

CAROL: Yes, it hurt terribly.

CLIFF: And I was as gentle as possible, Mrs Wilfred;
Because I've known such a mass to rupture during just
   such an examination.
You see,
If the material is allowed to stay inside and rot away,
The inflammation set up by all that rotting process
   going on in there seals everything tight.
Mrs Wilfred—I believe it's due to rupture in the near
   future.

CAROL: What happens then?

CLIFF: It's about as bad as can be, Mrs Wilfred.

CAROL: Do you make people happy, Doctor?

*(Room: DIVINA enters S R, crossing S L and up to window
corner.)*

CLIFF: I suppose so.

CAROL: Do you make them very happy?

CLIFF: Well, I try to.

CAROL: Do you make them happy with what you do
   with things—
With instruments, with tools, with—uh—
Or with some nefarious, uh...

(Rail: spot up on SHANNON *as, Sound: buzzer covers cut from "Planets" to "Tomorrow Tone.")*

SHANNON: No, I'm sorry—one down and nine to
   go—Miss Kilgallen!

(Office. fade out light. Room: lights up as SELDEN *enters S L; fade out spot.)*

Scene Forty-two

SELDEN: Divina?...
Say—what are you doing in here?
I've been looking all over for you.

(Room: SELDEN *crosses to S L edge of table as* DIVINA *crosses to S R edge.)*

DIVINA: Oh, I just figured I better lay low until you and
   Dad settled the football situation.

SELDEN: Yeah, your Dad is a regular guy.
And boy, is your mother a super cook!

DIVINA: Oh, when we go overboard, we really go
   overboard in this family.
The all-out Wilfreds, we're known as.

SELDEN: You're kidding, of course.
Well—guess I'll have to be traveling along—
Nice evening, Divina.
Sure glad I came over.

(Room: DIVINA *crosses center along downstage edge of table.)*

DIVINA: Are you, Selden?
I'm glad, too.

SELDEN: Yeah.
And thanks a lot for helping me.

DIVINA: That's all right, Selden, I—
I enjoyed helping you.

SELDEN: Yeah.
(Room: he crosses to DIVINA.*)*
I'm just sorry we never had any time to...

DIVINA: What?

SELDEN: Aw, nothing...

DIVINA: I didn't invite you over to make an
 incompleted pass, Selden.
I hope I haven't upset you.

SELDEN: What makes you think I blame you for
 anything?

DIVINA: But maybe I am to blame.
I tried so hard to fight against what I feel—
I didn't want you to know, ever!
You've been so...nice to me, but that's your nature.
It doesn't mean anything.

SELDEN: No, it means something.

DIVINA: Don't look so unhappy, Selden.
Don't worry about me.
I suppose no one ever...died of a broken heart....

(Room: they kiss; spot up on SHANNON *at rail as, Sound:
buzzer covers cut from "Tomorrow Tone" to "Planets.")*

SHANNON: Two down and eight to go—Mister
 Untermyer!

(Room: fade lights as, Office: lights reveal CLIFF *standing
behind desk,* CAROL *in patient's chair, S L.)*

Scene Forty-three

CAROL: You mean it's going to grow into a cancer?

CLIFF: No, Mrs Wilfred,
But its blood supply could be interfered with,
And it could break down and make you pretty sick,

And even if it didn't do that but just continued to grow,
It might become so large that it could interfere with
   other important internal organs—
It just grows like grass, Mrs Wilfred!

CAROL: And how...big could it get to be, Doctor?

CLIFF: The largest one I ever removed weighed fourteen
   pounds;
But I once saw one operated that weighed thirty-three—
You were a foolish woman—criminally foolish—
If you couldn't afford private medical attention, there
   are clinics!
You never would have got away with it in this town.

CAROL: How did you know it wasn't here that it
   happened?

CLIFF: Because it would have had to be reported to the
   Health Department,
And we follow up on such cases.

(Office: CAROL *bangs desk, leaps out of chair and turns off,
S L.)*

CAROL: I don't see what business it is of the Health
   Department!

(Office: CLIFF *sits behind desk.)*

CLIFF: We make it our business, Mrs Wilfred—
And it is a good thing, too—
For the protection of others as well as the one involved.
All you managed to do was let yourself in for years of
   trouble.

(Rail: spot up on SHANNON*)*

SHANNON: Now, I think it's only fair, Panel, so that you
   won't be misled,
To say that "No" would be the proper answer to that,
So it's three down and seven to go—Miss Francis!

(Rail: fade out spot. Office: CAROL *turns back to desk.)*

CAROL: But I'm so frightened, Doctor.

CLIFF: Good—
Now, we'll just have to make some preparations....

(Office: fade out lights. Room: lights reveal DIVINA *struggling in* SELDEN's *embrace.)*

Scene Forty-four

DIVINA: No...wait a minute!

SELDEN: Hey—what's happening?

DIVINA: No, Selden—stop it—let go of me!

SELDEN: Quit making such a big thing out of it—you
  ain't hurt!
(Room: embracing DIVINA, *he pushes her S R.)*

DIVINA: This is no good, Selden—it's just a sex
  attraction!

SELDEN: You're right—and name me something better!
You faker—don't you know what you really want?
Well, make up your mind, and make it up now,
Because I'm a restless guy!

(Room: SELDEN *kisses her; she breaks away.)*

DIVINA: Let's get something straight.
It'll save us both a lot of trouble in case we should ever
  run into each other again,
Which I promise you I shall try and avoid!
I think you're a stupid, vicious ape!

(Sound: slow crossfade from "Planets" to "Low Rumble")

DIVINA: Now, get out of my way!

SELDEN: You hadn't ought to talk to me like that, you
  know.
You hadn't ought to.

A girl ought to be friendly to a big football player.
You're just afraid to put out!

DIVINA: I'm just afraid of getting stuck with an ape like
   you.

SELDEN: You wouldn't mind that, you know—
They say that what the mother goes for,
The daughter goes for, too.

(*Room:* SELDEN *crosses to* DIVINA, *kisses her roughly,*
throws her to the floor and exits S L, taking his books off
table. DIVINA *runs off S R. Rail; spot up on* SHANNON.
Office: lights reveal CLIFF *with microphone at rail,*
S R side of office; CAROL *in S L chair.*)

Scene Forty-five

SHANNON: No, I'm sorry, Panel; but I'm going to flip
   over all the cards,
And let our challenger tell you just exactly what it is
   that he does....

(*Room:* SHANNON *exits up S R; spot out.*)

CLIFF: (*On mike*) Did you know Frank James as an
   outlaw?

CAROL: I couldn't be able to say definitely.
I assumed that he was, but I didn't know.

(*Sound: crossfade "Low Rumble" to "Piano Suspense"*)

CLIFF: Did you accept Peggy as an outlaw?

CAROL: I accepted Peggy as a friend.

CLIFF: Jimmy Ringo has testified that Frank James and
   Peggy were outlaws!

CAROL: I consider that slander and false.

CLIFF: Jimmy Ringo has testified about a meeting
In which Frank James passed information through
  Peggy on to Setank—
Do you recall such a meeting?

CAROL: There was never such a meeting—I deny it
  categorically.
I declare it is false!

CLIFF: Have you ever conspired or attempted to
transmit
Any secret information from any source to Setank?

CAROL: I have not.

(Office: CLIFF *crosses up to S R edge of desk; he places mike
in stand at S R edge and leans over it.)*

CLIFF: Was Frank James at that meeting?

CAROL: I will answer no more questions about that
  meeting.

CLIFF: Was Peggy there?

CAROL: I have refused to answer.

CLIFF: Was your daughter there?

CAROL: The same answer.
You can't infer that any person was or was not there!

CLIFF: Do you know Frank James?

CAROL: I have refused to answer.

CLIFF: Selden Clark?

CAROL: The same answer.

CLIFF: Your daughter?

CAROL: The same answer.

CLIFF: You refuse to say whether you know your own
  daughter?!

(Sound: crossfade "Piano Suspense" to "Low Rumble")

CAROL: I refuse because it would be helping in a fishing
   expedition.
Experience has taught me about fishing expeditions
   such as these.

(Office: CLIFF *crosses S L to* CAROL.*)*

CLIFF: Are any of these people outlaws or outlaw
sympathizers?

(Office: CLIFF *puts* CAROL *on mike.)*

CAROL: I think I'd like to talk to my family doctor,
   Doctor Sinclair.

CLIFF: Do, Mrs Wilfred!
I'll get him on the phone and explain what I've found,
And then let you talk to him....

(Office: CLIFF *exits S L; fade lights. Room:* DIVINA *as*
MISS PEGGY *enters S R crossing S L to center, followed
by* JASON *as* JIMMY RINGO.*)*

Scene Forty-six

JASON: What you do outside is your own business,
But this is our home!
How could you do this to us?
Am I to believe that you had so little regard for our
   feelings,
Or for principle,
Or for memory?

DIVINA: Are you completely blind to yourself, Dad?

JASON: I suppose you intend to explain that remark?

DIVINA: With all your talk of purity and honor,
Don't you really know what you want?
If you were only open and honest, it would be less
   horrible.
You make me feel unclean!

(Room: JASON *draws his gun.)*

JASON: All right, up with your hands!

DIVINA: Have you lost your mind?

(Room: DIVINA *walks S R past* JASON, *turning him around;* JASON *gestures with gun, then puts it away.)*

JASON: You're an outlaw, ain't you?
Well, I'm taking you prisoner!

(Sound: add "Indian Raid" to "Low Rumble" and swell. Room: SELDEN *as* FRANK, *wearing a poncho that conceals his hands, enters S L and crosses down S L.)*

JASON: You will confine yourself to quarters pending
  further orders.

SELDEN: You're not going to hold a white woman here
  in the face of an Indian attack, are you, Mister Ringo?

(Room: JASON *holds his hands up.)*

JASON: Miss Peggy's safety is my responsibility,
  stranger.

SELDEN: Miss Peggy is my fiancée, Mr Ringo.

(Room: JASON *turns to face* SELDEN.)*

SELDEN: And there's another thing you ought to know:
Those two Indian braves you shot were Setank's sons—
He doesn't want the rest of us—
It's your scalp he's after!

JASON: What's your real name, boy?

(Room: JASON *and* SELDEN *square off.)*

SELDEN: He's closing in on all sides, Pop—
That doesn't matter anymore.

JASON: It matters to me—you're Frank James, ain't you?

SELDEN: That's right—you heard of me?

JASON: Yeah, I heard about you, you miserable outlaw.
I heard you're a cheap, no good, barroom loafer!
And now I'm going to stand you up and shoot you.

(Room: DIVINA *crosses S L to* SELDEN, *embracing him.)*

DIVINA: I never wanted it to end this way, Frank.

SELDEN: There never was any other way, Peggy—
We just put it off a while....

DIVINA: Oh, Frank...

JASON: Stand clear, Miss Peggy, or I'll have to shoot you
too!

(Room: with left hand SELDEN *moves* DIVINA *up S L.)*

SELDEN: You mean, you'd shoot an unarmed woman
down in cold blood, Pop?

JASON: You're asking for trouble, son.

(Room: SELDEN *holds out right hand, under poncho.)*

SELDEN: And you already got it, Mister—
'Cause I got a gun on you and it's pointed smack at
your belly!

(Room: SELDEN *crosses slowly S R towards* JASON.
DIVINA *crosses against upstage wall to center. Sound:*
CLIFF *speaks from off S R mike.)*

CLIFF: *(Off)* Mrs Wilfred...?

JASON: I ought to blow your head off for laying for me
like that!

CAROL: *(On S L desk mike)* Yes, Doctor?

SELDEN: These new .45's really put a hole in a man,
Jimmy—
Now, you gonna clear out of here or not?

CLIFF: *(Off)* Why don't you unburden your mind and
clear your conscience by telling us the full story?

(Room: JASON *raises both hands.)*

JASON: If I didn't have something else on my mind,
I'd take them guns away from you and slap you
  cross-eyed!

CAROL: *(On mike)* Yes. Yes, why don't I...
After all...

SELDEN: Why don't I just stroke you one across the
  snout!

(Room: SELDEN *pulls back poncho to reveal he's been bluffing
with a bare hand. Both men drop into gunfighter's crouch
and back away. Their challenges overlap with* CAROL's
confession in office, over S L desk mike.)

Scene Forty-seven

CAROL:
I was engaged in
espionage from the middle
of 1942 until about a year
ago. There was a
continuous passing of
information relating to
atomic energy at irregular
but frequent meetings.
This illegal association
commenced at my own
initiative, and no approach
had been made to me. I
myself spoke to an
intermediary who arranged
the first interview. This
was in a private house,
where I met a man whom I
believed to be Russian.

JASON:
Are you prepared to back
  up that remark or not?

SELDEN:
How'd you like to try
  and make me?

JASON:
I want to know what you
  meant by that remark
  you just passed

This was early in 1942.
After this first meeting,
there were two or three
meetings for about six
months before I went to
Delray Beach in
December, 1943. The
talks were sometimes
certainly with Russians,
but others were with
persons of unknown
nationalities. There was a
prearranged rendezvous
and recognition signals
were exchanged.
Generally the meetings
were of short duration, and
consisted of my passing
documentary information,
and with the other party
arranging the next
rendezvous. At times I
was questioned, but I
thought it to have been
inspired from some other
quarter than my contact. I
realized that I was carrying
my life in my hands, but I
had done this from the
time of my underground
days in Germany. I said I
still believed in
Communism, but not as
practiced in Russia today.

SELDEN:
Why don't you button up
    your britches and go
    home?

JASON:
I'm warning you, Frank—
    I'm going to get you!

SELDEN:
Yeah, I know—I heard that
    one before, too.

JASON:
I won't just try it, I'll do it!
I got my mind made up,
    now!

SELDEN:
Then quit talking about it,
    Mister, and go for your
    guns!

(Offstage: string of firecrackers explodes stage: JASON *and* SELDEN *fall down;* DIVINA *hides under table. Office:* CAROL *rises and exits S L. Window:* CLIFF *as* LIBDER *enters S R, speaking into "instrument;"* SHANNON *as* HUDRAY *enters S L.)*

Scene Forty-eight

CLIFF: Poskon calling Corplum!
Poskon calling Corplum!
Come in, Corplum, over—
Come in, Corplum!
Can't contact them—they won't answer!

SHANNON: Of course they will—everything will be all
    right!
We must report everything—tell them as much as we
    can!

CLIFF: No—it's hopeless—we're lost—everything's lost!
Now Corplum will never know the terrible truths that
    we learned!

(Offstage: second string of firecrackers explodes. Room: JASON *and* SELDEN, *who have struggled to their feet, fall down again. Window:* CLIFF *is hit by gunfire; falls.)*

CLIFF: Murdering savages!

SHANNON: No, Libder—they are crazed, despairing
    wretches!
Pity them! Pity them!
(Window: SHANNON *takes "instrument" from* CLIFF.*)*
Poskon calling Corplum!
Poskon calling Corplum!
Come in, Corplum, over—
Come in, Corplum

(Offstage: third string of firecrackers explodes. Window:
SHANNON *is hit by gunfire. Room:* JASON *and* SELDEN, *who
have struggled to their feet, fall down again. Fade to blackout)*

*(Sound: crossfade from "Indian Raid" and "Low Rumble"
to "Mood 2." Room: spot on* DIVINA, *as she crawls out
from under table and crosses down center to rail.)*

Scene Forty-nine

DIVINA: One moment they were all around us, and we
   were drowning in Indians;
Then suddenly, it was over with,
And we had the desert to ourselves.

(Room: JASON *exits S R,* SELDEN *exits S L. Window:*
CLIFF *and* SHANNON *exit.)*

DIVINA: So we just ran—
Past the station and over the bridge between the
   boundaries and the railroad tracks,
While the light changed from gray to pale green then
   back to gold,
Over the ascending monolith of General Hospital,
Leaving the ugly industrial section,
Past endless honey and olive and french-fried almond
   stands,
Past the acrid smell of dairies and the white silt of
   quarries,
Past Mexican restaurants with their promise of hot
   tamales,
Past Moorish motels with their promise of hot nights,
And at our left, canceling out all the ugliness.
Those incredible papier-mache mountains,
Their dawn-stained peaks gradually reddening while
   the round metal ball of the morning sun moved
   gradually up from behind like a disk spewed forth
   from some gigantic blast furnace—

(Rail: DIVINA *crosses S R, as, Room: lights up;* CAROL *in bathrobe enters S L and crosses center behind table as, Office:* JASON *enters S L, crosses S R behind desk to watch* CAROL; *then* CLIFF *enters S L.)*

DIVINA: Miles and miles and miles of this—
Until we entered the Robot Era of 2150,
Where almost every morning, winter or summer,
Jason and Carol Wilfred waken to sunlight streaming
   through the pale-gray and aqua bedroom
Of their Delray Beach, Florida, home....

(Room: DIVINA *exits S R. Office:* JASON *turns to* CLIFF.)*

JASON: Is she going to be all right?

CLIFF: I don't know, Mister Wilfred.
She's hurt pretty bad.

(Sound: crossfade "Mood 2" to "Slow Remorse." Room: CAROL *straightens table and chairs.)*

CAROL: *(Out)* ...happened to see Europe again was...
...that trip to the end is coming here tomorrow after the
   packages arrived...
...yesterday brought good cheer as...
...after my release, I was asked to help Professor R E
   Peierels on some war work...

(Office: JASON *crosses around desk down S L.)*

CLIFF: I guess she had nothing left to live for....

CAROL: *(Out)* I accepted it without knowing what the
   work was,
But I doubt if it would have made any difference to my
   subsequent actions if I had.

JASON: But didn't she give you any explanation at all?

CAROL: *(Out)* You see, if you believe in Sackoy,
You are a good person.

CLIFF: What explanation could she give that you don't already know?

(Office: CLIFF *exits S L. Window:* SELDEN *as* FRANK *and* DIVINA *as* MISS PEGGY *enter S L, crossing S R.)*

DIVINA: One battle, and there's so much work to be done.

SELDEN: Yes, but look at them—
Already they're starting to rebuild.

CAROL: *(Out)* In the course of this work, I naturally began to form bonds of personal friendship,
And I had to conceal them from my own thoughts.
I used my Marxian philosophy to conceal my thoughts in two separate compartments....

DIVINA: Is it true what the courier said:
That the war will soon be over?

SELDEN: Yes.

DIVINA: Doesn't the end of the war have to be a beginning?

CAROL: *(Out)* Some people don't like Sackoy,
But I could be free and easy with other people, because they don't like to be punished,
And I knew the other compartment would step in if I reached a danger point.

SELDEN: *Mejores mañanas passaran.*

CAROL: *(Out)* Looking back on it now,
I would call it controlled schizophrenia.

DIVINA: What does that mean?

SELDEN: It means: It'll all seem better tomorrow.

DIVINA: Tomorrow...

(Window: DIVINA *and* SELDEN *cross S R to exit.*
Office: JASON *exits S L.)*

DIVINA: ...Sure does have a pretty sound....

CAROL: Go—it will be pleasant for you when I am near
   the table in the dining room was crowded with people
   it crashed into were screaming that they had been—
You see,
I still believed that Russia would build a new world,
And that I would take part in it.
The earth would be a vast garden.
National boundaries would be obsolete, and language
   barriers a thing of the past.
(Room: she crosses down S R to rail.)
There would be no threats of war.
Hospitals and prisons would be almost empty.
Trips to the moon would be commonplace;
And the crowded cities of today would have
   disappeared—
In their place, communities planned for better living:
Men and machines together doing the work and play of
   the world,
Reaching toward an ever-greater harmony,
And orderliness,
And beauty....

(Room: CLIFF *as* LIBDER *and* SHANNON *as* HUDRAY *enter
S L;* SHANNON *crosses very slowly down S R to* CAROL,
who turns to face her; then SHANNON *slowly backs up
S L again.)*

Scene Fifty

CLIFF: Whatever you dream, believe the opposite....

SHANNON: Dreams go by opposites....

CLIFF: If you dream of a funeral or a death...

SHANNON: It is a sure sign of a wedding...

CLIFF: If you dream of a marriage...

SHANNON: It is a sign of death...

CLIFF: If you dream of the dead...

SHANNON: You will hear from the living...

CLIFF: If you dream of a flower...

SHANNON: It is a sign of death.

CLIFF: If you dream of a snake, you have an enemy.

SHANNON: If you dream of a fire, you have an enemy.

CLIFF: To dream of a snake that you do not kill
Is a sign that you have an active enemy.

SHANNON: Dream a thing three times,
And the dream will come true.

(Room: CAROL crosses slowly up left toward CLIFF and SHANNON.)

BOTH: If a person starts to say something to you and
then forgets what he is going to say...

SHANNON: It is a lie.

BOTH: If your shoe comes untied someone is thinking...

CLIFF: About you.

BOTH: If you go to sleep with the moon on your face
you will...

SHANNON: Go insane.

(Room: SHANNON and CLIFF turn up S L as CAROL walks past them and exits up S L.)

SHANNON: When a child walks backwards...

CLIFF: It is cursing its parents.

(Slow fade to blackout)

END OF PLAY

New York City, 20 June 1985

www.ingramcontent.com/pod-product-compliance
Lightning Source LLC
Chambersburg PA
CBHW070020110426
42741CB00034B/2259